Popular How-to-Use Chords

Easy-to-Use • Easy-to-Carry
Internet Audio Links

Jake Jackson

T0364381
9781787552982

**FLAME TREE
PUBLISHING**

Publisher and Creative Director: Nick Wells
Project Editor: Gillian Whitaker
Layout Design: Jane Ashley
Musical Examples & Recordings: Phil Dawson

19 21 23 22 20
1 3 5 7 9 10 8 6 4 2

This edition first published 2019 by
FLAME TREE PUBLISHING
6 Melbray Mews
London SW6 3NS
United Kingdom
www.flametreepublishing.com
Music website: www.flametreemusic.com

© 2019 Flame Tree Publishing Ltd

ISBN 978-1-78755-298-2

A CIP record for this book is available from the British Library upon request.

Acknowledgements
All images and diagrams © Flame Tree Publishing, except the following: Shutterstock.com and courtesy Sydneymills 6; Tyler Olson 11; Dean Drobot 27; SunnyGraph 49; Mr.Whiskey 52; Pepsco Studio 57; Jiinna 65; panitanphoto 111, 381; Africa Studio 153; aodaodaodaod 155; Piotr Piatrouski 157, 347; 4 PM production 208; Beauty Studio 211; LightField Studios 213, 313; COZ 221; Christopher Hall 249; Robby Fontanesi 258; 88studio 261; Lukas Gojda 263; MaxShutter 271; Oleh Slepchenko 299; Pavel L Photo and Video 308; Milan Ilic Photographer 311; Viktoriia Hnatiuk 357. Android, iPhone, iPad, Nokia, Samsung and Galaxy S are all trademarks or registered trademarks.

Jake Jackson is a musician and writer of practical music books. He has created and contributed to over 30 practical music books, including *How to Play Guitar* and the bestselling *Guitar Chord* and *Piano Chord* titles.

Phil Dawson (musical examples/recordings) is a guitarist, composer and teacher whose work encompasses a variety of touring, recording, film and TV work as an instrumentalist, bandleader, music writer and producer. He's also a lecturer and mentor at a variety of educational levels, and devisor of several courses for instrumentalists, bands and studio musicians. See his work at www.phildawsonmusic.co.uk.

Printed in China

Contents

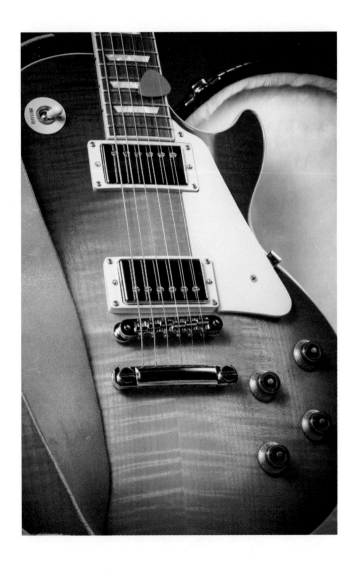

Introduction

In music, knowledge of just a few common chords can get you a long way. Many songs consist of a short chord sequence that is repeated throughout, often using similar chord types that are popular because of the way they sound together. Familiarity with the ways in which you can use these main chords can therefore help you learn a range of songs, play along with others, and experiment with creating your own music.

Designed for both guitar and piano, this book will take you through this process by introducing the most popular chords and the variety of different ways they can be used. To give a brief overview of the chapters in this book:

Chapter 1 provides quick guides to the chord diagrams and musical notation you will find in this book. It also shows you how to access the accompanying online audio for the chords and examples at flametreemusic.com.

Chapter 2 outlines the basic principles behind chords and the most important ones in relation to keys and scales. Also includes tips on chord playing techniques for the guitar and piano, and introduces chord charts and chord combinations.

Chapter 3 offers a reference library of guitar and piano chord diagrams for the main keys. You will find major and minor triads, and dominant 7th, major 7th and minor 7th chords for C, D, E, F, G, A and B.

Chapter 4 kicks things off with the I V vi IV progression, showing it in use in C, D, E, G and A. Chord diagrams, examples and variations are provided, with accompanying audio samples.

Chapter 5 does the same for the I IV V progression, with examples (and links to the audio online) showing the progression in the main keys. Demonstrated variations include added 7ths, the twelve-bar blues, and the minor i iv V.

Chapter 6 shows how to use the ii V I progression in the main keys, and with variations, including examples and audio links throughout.

Chapter 7 covers the I vi IV V progression. Again, examples are given of it in common keys and with variations, including links and online audio.

Chapter 8 gives further ideas on embellishing your chords and chord progressions, including using extended and altered chords, chord substitution and moving bass lines.

Chapter 9 builds on previous chapters by advising on how to bring everything together to develop your music. Here you'll find an introduction to basic song structure and techniques for soloing over chords.

Chapter 10 lists a few of our other music resources including companion books in the series and our website flametreemusic.com.

1

1

Before You Begin

Thoughout this book, chord diagrams and
examples are provided for both guitar and
piano. This chapter shows how the diagrams
are laid out and how they link to audio online
at flametreemusic.com. It also gives a reminder
of fretboard and keyboard notes, chord symbols,
and standard and TAB notation.

1

Fretboard & Keyboard

The Fretboard

When dealing with chords it's useful to have a clear idea of where each note lies in relation to other notes. On the guitar, the frets are organized in semitone intervals:

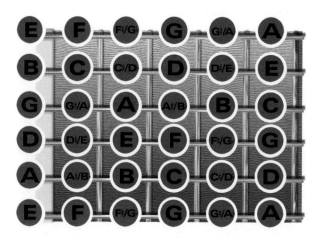

Guitar fingerboard with nut on the left, bass strings at the bottom, high E string at the top

The Keyboard

On the piano, each note is next to notes either a semitone above or a semitone below it. Higher notes are on the right; lower notes are on the left.

The black keys on the keyboard are sharps (♯) and flats (♭). For example, in the diagram below, between C and D there is a note called either C♯ or D♭. It is referred to as either of these names dependent on the context of the other notes.

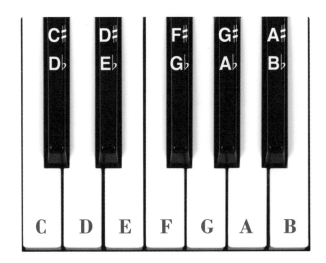

Chord Diagrams: Guitar

The bass E appears on the left (6th string)

The top E is on the right (1st string)

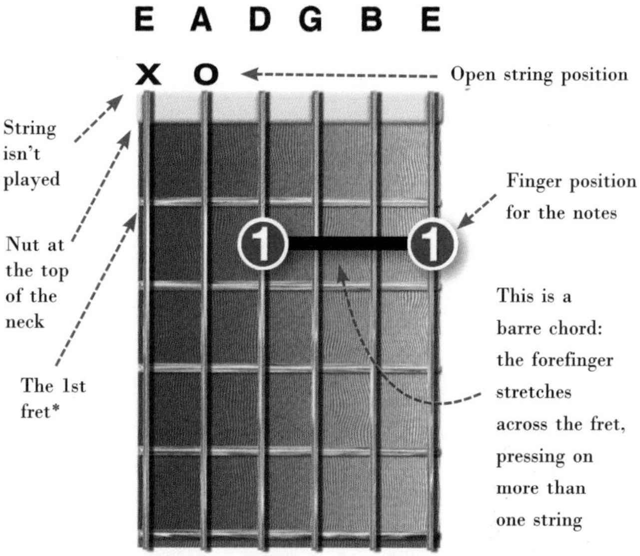

E   A   D   G   B   E

X   O ◄- - - - - - - - - - - - Open string position

String isn't played

Finger position for the notes

Nut at the top of the neck

This is a barre chord: the forefinger stretches across the fret, pressing on more than one string

The 1st fret*

A6

1 is the index finger   **2** is the middle finger

3 is the ring finger   **4** is the little finger

* When the chord position isn't as close to the nut, a number to the left indicates the changed location on the fretboard. E.g. a '2' means the diagram starts from the 2nd fret rather than the 1st.

Chord Diagrams: Piano

Finger positions

Throughout the book the fingers are given numbers:

For the Left Hand: ① is the thumb   ② is the index finger
③ is the middle finger   ④ is the ring finger
⑤ is the little finger

For the Right Hand: ① is the thumb   ② is the index finger
③ is the middle finger   ④ is the ring finger
⑤ is the little finger

Chord name
and type ---------→

Tabs down
the side to
locate chapter

C
Major

Suggested
fingering

QR code
link to
chord
online

Starting ---------→
note of the
diagram

Chord Spelling
1st (C), 3rd (E), 5th (G)

15

Standard Notation

In this book there are several instances where chords are shown in practice, as part of a piece of short music. While some musical knowledge is assumed, the below is provided as a quick reminder of how music is recorded in standard musical notation.

Treble Clef

The pitch of a note is indicated by where it is positioned on the musical stave. The clef tells you which range of pitches the notes on the stave represent. The guitar and the right hand on the piano both generally use the treble clef.

C C♯ D D♯ E F F♯ G G♯ A A♯ B

Bass Clef

The range represented by the treble clef mostly applies to notes above middle C. For notes below middle C, the bass clef is used. It is usually used for the left hand on the piano.

A range of notes represented by the bass clef include:

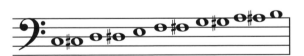

C C♯ D D♯ E F F♯ G G♯ A A♯ B

1

TAB Notation

Some guitarists prefer to use tablature (called TAB) instead of staves.

The six lines represent the six strings of the guitar, from the high E string to the low E string, and the numbers represent the frets that produce the notes. A zero indicates that the string is played open.

In the below example, the first C is played on the 5th string – the A string – by holding down the third fret along. The D is produced by playing the 4th string open, the E is sounded by holding down the second fret on the same string, then the third fret on the same string produces the F, and so on.

```
T                                           0 — 1
A                             0 — 2
B                 0 — 2 — 3
      3
      C    D    E    F    G    A    B    C
```

The examples shown in this book show chord progressions using both standard (treble clef) and TAB notation.

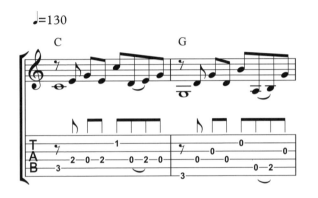

In the above example, you can see how the length of the notes is shown in both treble and TAB staves.

Not all of the notes in the examples will be the same length, so the next two pages provide a brief overview of how different note lengths are notated.

1

Rhythm Notation

Chords can be communicated a number of different ways in music. As well as simple chord charts (see page 60), they can be shown in rhythm charts, and full musical notation, both of which specify particular note durations.

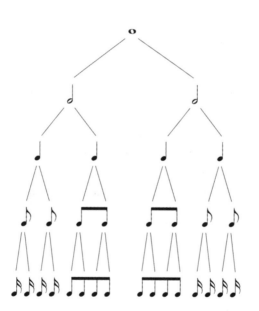

These note values also have an equivalent rest. Here's a quick reminder of the note names and rest symbols, with their relative lengths:

NAME	NOTE	REST	DURATION IN 4/4 TIME
Semibreve (whole note)	o	▬	4 beats
Dotted Minim	♩.	▬·	3 beats
Minim (half note)	♩	▬	2 beats
Dotted Crotchet	♩.	𝄽.	1½ beats
Crotchet (quarter note)	♩	𝄽	1 beat
Dotted Quaver	♪.	𝄾.	¾ beat
Quaver (eighth note)	♪	𝄾	½ beat
Semiquaver (sixteenth note)	♬	𝄿	¼ beat

You may also come across ties (a curved line joining two notes of the same pitch) and triplets (where 3 notes are played in the space of 2 notes of the same value).

Sound Links

You'll need an internet-ready smartphone with a camera (e.g. iPhone, any Android phone (e.g. Samsung Galaxy, Nokia Lumia). The best results are achieved using a **WIFI** connection.

1. With the most recent phone software updates you can **use the camera to scan**. If this doesn't work you can download **any free QR code reader** from your phone's app store.

2. On your smartphone, open the app and scan the QR code whenever it appears in this book.

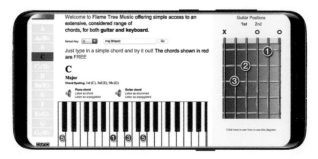

3. This will take you directly to the relevant chord or example on **flametreemusic.com**, where you can access and **hear** a huge library of sounds.

4. Use the drop-down menu to choose from 20 scales or **12 free chords** (50 with subscription) **per key.**

5. Click the sounds! Both piano and guitar audio is provided for whole chords and individual notes.

6. The music examples throughout this book appear in a special menu on flametreemusic.com where you can **hear the whole example.** You'll need to register with the last four digits of the ISBN of this book (2982).

1

Chord Symbols

There are two main types of chords that form the core of most popular music: major chords and minor chords. Major chords have a bright, strong sound and minor chords have a mellow, sombre sound.

The chord symbol for major chords is simply the letter name of the chord written as a capital. For example, the chord symbol for the G major chord is 'G'.

Minor chord symbols consist of the capital letter of the chord name followed by a lowercase 'm'. For example, the chord symbol for the E minor chord is 'Em'.

Other chord types tend to just extend or vary the notes of the major or minor triads using other notes from the key. Opposite is a list of common chord types and their symbols shown for the key of C.

Chord Name	Chord Symbol	Chord Notes
C major	**C**	C, E, G
C minor	**Cm**	C, E♭, G
C augmented triad	**C+**	C, E, G♯
C diminished triad	**C°**	C, E♭, G♭
C suspended 2nd	**Csus2**	C, D, G
C suspended 4th	**Csus4**	C, F, G
C 5th (power) chord	**C5**	C, G
C major 6th	**C6**	C, E, G, A
C minor 6th	**Cm6**	C, E♭, G, A
C dominant 7th	**C7**	C, E, G, B♭
C major 7th	**Cmaj7**	C, E, G, B
C minor 7th	**Cm7**	C, E♭, G, B♭
C half diminished 7th	**C⌀7 or Cm7♭5**	C, E♭, G♭, B♭
C diminished 7th	**C°7**	C, E♭, G♭, B♭♭
C minor major 7th	**Cm(maj7)**	C, E♭, G, B
C dominant 7th ♯5	**C7+5**	C, E, G♯, B♭
C dominant 7th ♭5	**C7♭5**	C, E, G♭, B♭
C major add 9	**Cadd9**	C, E, G, D
C dominant 9th	**C9**	C, E, G, B♭, D
C major 9th	**Cmaj9**	C, E, G, B, D
C minor 9th	**Cm9**	C, E♭, G, B♭, D
C dominant 11th	**C11**	C, E, G, B♭, D, F
C dominant 13th	**C13**	C, E, G, B♭, D, A

2

The Basics

When combining chords, if you have a clear knowledge of the chords involved and how they relate to one another it will be easier to adapt to new keys, new structures, and new musical ideas. By developing the right playing technique too, chord transitions and unfamiliar chords will be easier to master.

Chords, Keys & Scales

The harmonic links that exist between notes are central to understanding which notes will sound good together, and which won't.

A **chord** simply refers to different notes sounded together. In their most basic form, chords are formed of three notes, called a triad.

The **key** of a song refers to its overall tonality, and tells you which scale will be used as the basis of its melody and which chords fit naturally within it.

A **scale** is a set of ordered pitches in a key. Different scales produce different tonalities, but they follow patterns that can be applied to each key.

An **interval** is the distance between each pitch, usually counted in steps and half-steps, or tones and semitones.

To understand the key of a piece of music it helps to look at its scale, as this organizes all the key's notes into pitch order.

The Major Scale

Different scales produce different tonalities, but they follow patterns that can be applied to each key. The patterns take the form of a set order of tones (whole steps) and semitones (half-steps). The combination of these tells you the distance (or 'interval') between each pitch. By far the most important scale in music is the major scale, which always follows the same pattern:

T   T   S   T   T   T   S

When this pattern is applied to the key of C, it will produce the C major scale. Starting with C, a tone (T) up from C is D, then a tone up from D is E, then a semitone (S) from E is F, and so on:

C   D   E   F   G   A   B   C

The intervals between each note and the key note are called a '2nd', a '3rd', a '4th' etc. The octave marks the point where the key's seven scale notes are repeated.

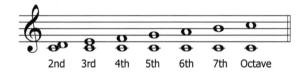

2nd   3rd   4th   5th   6th   7th   Octave

The type of 'quality' of each interval is dependent on the number of semitones involved. For example, in major scales there are 4 semitones between the root note and the 3rd: this is called a major third.

If the interval distance is altered, this changes the tonality and overall 'status' of the interval. When 'major' intervals drop a semitone, they become 'minor'.

Major scales contain all the same interval qualities:

C to D	=	Major Second
C to E	=	Major Third
C to F	=	Perfect Fourth
C to G	=	Perfect Fifth
C to A	=	Major Sixth
C to B	=	Major Seventh

For example, if E here is lowered to an E♭ (from 4 to 3 semitones), its relationship to the key note is a minor 3rd. Similarly, if the major 7th lowers from the B to B♭, the interval becomes a minor 7th.

The C major scale in standard and TAB notation looks like:

Any chords in this key are derived from these seven notes.

Constructing Chords

Chords are created by combining notes of various intervals. Major chords, for example, are based on a major third interval.

It is common to number notes in a scale using Roman numerals, which refer to the note's position in the scale as well as the type of chord derived from it.

An uppercase numeral means a chord built on that note is major; lowercase represents a minor chord.

So the scale of C major could be written as:

C	D	E	F	G	A	B
I	ii	iii	IV	V	vi	vii°
1st	2nd	3rd	4th	5th	6th	7th
Major	Minor	Minor	Major	Major	Minor	Diminished

The 1st, 3rd and 5th notes of the major scale make up its major triad. So the C major triad contains the notes C, E and G.

Using the same method to form triads for each note of this major scale would give us a harmonized version of the C major scale. This shows us that the following chords are all within the key of C:

I:	C	(C, E, G)
ii:	Dm	(D, F, A)
iii:	Em	(E, G, B)
IV:	F	(F, A, C)
V:	G	(G, B, D)
vi:	Am	(A, C, E)
vii°:	B°	(B, D, F)

On the guitar, although triads only contain three different notes, strumming three-string chords can result in quite a thin sound. Often chord notes are doubled so that five or six strings can be strummed.

Playing Chords –
Techniques for Guitar

Hand Positions

Whether playing chords or single notes, press the fretting-hand fingers as close to the fretwire as possible. Try to keep all fretting-hand fingers close to the fingerboard to minimize the amount of movement.

Using a Plectrum

If you're using a plectrum/pick, grip it between the index finger and thumb. Position it so that its tip extends just beyond the fingertip, by about 1/10 in (2.5 mm). Hold it with a small amount of pressure.

Strumming Techniques

When strumming chords, let the action come from the wrist rather than the elbow, and keep the wrist, elbow and shoulder loose and relaxed. Don't over-grip with the fretting-hand thumb on the back of the neck.

Barre Chords

Playing a barre chord involves re-fingering an open position chord so as to leave the first finger free to play the barre by fretting all six strings. The whole chord can then be moved up the fingerboard to different pitches. Using barre chords will also allow you to play more unusual chords (like B♭ minor or F♯ major), which are unobtainable in open position.

They're a bit trickier to play than open chords, so here are some tips to keep in mind:

- Keep the first finger straight and in line with the fret.
- Position all the fretting fingers as close to the fretwire as possible. Press down firmly, but avoid using excessive pressure.
- When you move between barre chords ensure that your thumb also shifts, so that your whole hand position is moving with each chord change.

Playing Chords – Techniques for Piano

Hand Positions

For piano playing, keep your nails reasonably short but do not over-do it. Play the keys with the part of your finger between the tip and the pad.

Your fingers should curve gently on to the keys. Avoid straight fingers, but do not curl them up too much. Imagine your hand is a spider which needs to run along the keyboard. You can go much faster if your fingers are curved and relaxed.

To get an ideal position, try letting a tennis ball rest in the palm of your hand, with your fingers touching it all round. Relax a little, remove the ball and turn your hand over: this is the position you need.

When playing chords, ensure you have all fingers in the correct place before pressing down on them all at the same time.

To indicate when a particular finger should play a note, each finger is given a number. That way, if a note should be played with the middle finger you would see a number 3 above the note on the music.

Both hands have their thumb and fingers numbered from 1 to 5, starting with the thumb.

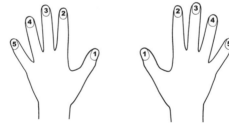

These numbers appear in notation above or below the note. In this book's chord diagrams, suggested fingerings for the right hand are shown in red circles.

Important Chords

Not only does a scale tell you which notes are in a key, but the position of a note in a scale also alerts you to its importance in that key.

For example, the first degree ('tonic') is usually central to establishing the tonality of the section.

The V note (the 'dominant') is also important due to its strong harmonic relationship with the tonic. So in the key of C major, G occupies an important function and position in relation to C. Another tonally important degree of the scale is the IV (the 'subdominant').

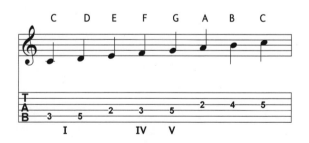

Chords built on these degrees are the key's primary chords: the most important and definitive chords for that key. When putting together chord progressions from major scales, then, using these establishes a strong sense of key and will sound more natural.

The I, IV and V chords of a key are all major chords, which is why they sound so strong when in that key.

Major chords consist of a major third interval, which is the distance from the first to the third note of the major scale e.g. in the key of C, from C to E.

Major 3rd

1	2	**3**	4	**5**	6	7
C	D	**E**	F	**G**	A	B

Common Chords in C

As well as the I, IV and V chords, other useful chords in the key include the ii and vi chords, which are frequently found in chord progressions too.

The ii and vi are minor chords, as indicated by the lower case Roman numerals. Just as the major third interval determines that a chord has a major tonality, a minor third interval determines that a chord is minor. Minor thirds are just 3 semitones from the root note. If you lower the major third interval by a half step it becomes a minor third.

The C minor chord takes its notes from the C natural minor scale:

1	2	3	4	5	6	7
C	D	E♭	F	G	A♭	B♭

These most common chords are shown below in C, in standard and TAB notation.

C Major Scale

C	D	E	F	G	A	B
I	ii	iii	IV	V	vi	vii°

I – C Major
Notes: C, E, G

V – G Major
Notes: G, B, D

IV – F Major
Notes: F, A, C

ii – D Minor
Notes: D, F, A

vi – A Minor
Notes: A, C, E

Common Chords in Other Keys

C major isn't the only key that's used in music. Other common keys include D major, E major, G major and A major.

Scales are based on patterns on the keyboard or fretboard, and can be transposed by moving that pattern up or down the keyboard or fretboard.

All we need to do to find a major scale in another key is to apply the pattern to that starting note:

T   T   S   T   T   T   S

So, if this time we start on D, we would get the D major scale:

Using Roman numerals, you can quickly find the key's most important chords. The I chord would take D as its root, with the 3rd and 5th to complete the triad: D, F#, A. The V chord would take G as its root, forming the triad again using notes from the scale: G, B, D.

Although there are no fixed rules about which chords can be combined when you are composing a song or chord progression, if you select chords from the same key they will always fit together well.

The following pages provide a reference for the most common chords in the most common keys.

Common Chords of the D Major Scale

D Major Scale

D	E	F♯	G	A	B	C♯
I	ii	iii	IV	V	vi	vii°

I – D Major

Notes: D, F♯, A

V – A Major

Notes: A, C♯, E

IV – G Major

Notes: G, B, D

ii – E Minor

Notes: E, G, B

vi – B Minor

Notes: B, D, F♯

Common Chords of the E Major Scale

D Major Scale

E	F#	G#	A	B	C#	D#
I	ii	iii	IV	V	vi	vii°

I – E Major
Notes: E, G#, B

V – B Major
Notes: B, D#, F#

IV – A Major
Notes: A, C#, E

ii – F# Minor
Notes: F#, A, C#

vi – C# Minor
Notes: C#, E, G#

Common Chords of the G Major Scale

G Major Scale

G	A	B	C	D	E	F♯
I	ii	iii	IV	V	vi	vii°

I – G Major

Notes: G, B, D

V – D Major

Notes: D, F♯, A

IV – C Major

Notes: C, E, G

ii – A Minor

Notes: A, C, E

vi – E Minor

Notes: E, G, B

Common Chords of the A Major Scale

A Major Scale

A	B	C#	D	E	F#	G#
I	ii	iii	IV	V	vi	vii°

I – A Major
Notes: A, C#, E

V – E Major
Notes: E, G#, B

IV – D Major
Notes: D, F#, A

ii – B Minor
Notes: B, D, F#

vi – F# Minor
Notes: F#, A, C#

47

Putting Chords Together

When playing chords it's important to learn how to change fluently between them without leaving gaps. This can be a difficult skill to master, but luckily there are a few shortcuts you can take.

Minimum Movement Principle

It's essential that chord changes are crisp, prompt, and in time. This can be made easier if following the 'minimum movement principle', which involves making only the smallest finger movement necessary between chords, and avoiding taking fingers off notes or frets only to put them back on again for the next chord.

Excess movement between chords is what slows chord changes down; the less your fingers move, the faster your chord changes will be.

Shared Notes

Always look for links, or common notes, between consecutive chords, so you can minimize the amount of finger movement needed when changing chords. You may be able to keep some fingers on, or at least slide them (on the guitar) along a string to the next chord.

Tips for Smooth Chord Transitions – Guitar

Strumming Technique

Upstrum: V   Downstrum: ⊓

An upstrum should be played by an upwards movement generated from the wrist, as though the strumming hand is almost effortlessly bouncing back into position ready for the next downstrum.

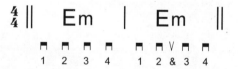

You can add another upstrum to each bar, to give one between beats two and three, and after the fourth beat. Next, try and keep the strumming pattern going through a chord change to A minor.

Fingerpicking Technique

An alternative to strumming, fingerpicking can add melodic interest to a chord progression.

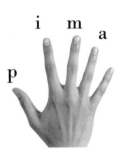

Each picking finger is identified by a letter:

p = thumb
i = index finger
m = middle finger
a = ring finger

Picking patterns nearly always begin by playing the root note of the chord on the bass string using the thumb. In the below example, the low E string would be the first note of the pattern.

Opposite you'll see a chord progression in A minor for the guitar. Between each new chord there's a return to the basic A minor chord.

Notice the common notes between the chords shown: the first finger stays on the first fret and the second finger stays on the second fret throughout.

• The open position A minor and F major chords both include the note C (first fret on the B string).

• The C major chord also includes this note, and, in addition, has another note in common with

the A minor chord (E on the second fret of the D string). Between Am and C only the third finger needs to be moved.

- Notice, too, how E major is the same 'shape' as Am – just on different strings.

'Open Vamp' Strum

If all else fails, this is a 'pro-trick' you can use that will mask any gap between chord changes.

This simply involves strumming the open strings while your fingers move between the chord change. It's not ideal, but it does maintain fluency and some players make it a feature to bring out accents.

Power Chords

In rock music, instead of full chords, abbreviated versions just using the root and fifth note are often played. Apart from the tone, one of the main advantages of using these 'power chords' is that it's much easier to move quickly from chord to chord because there are only a couple of fingers involved. To play a fifth power chord, simply fret a note on any bass string and add a note two frets up on the adjacent higher string.

Sliding Chords

The guitar is one of the few instruments on which you can slide chords up and down, changing their pitch easily and smoothly. This creates a fluidity and smoothness of sound, and forms a core component of rhythm-guitarist's technique.

When sliding chords it's important to ensure that the chord shape is maintained, so that one finger doesn't end up a fret ahead of the rest. Keep the chord shape under control, whilst keeping the fingers relaxed enough to slide up or down the fretboard.

In TAB notation, sliding chords are usually shown using an 'S' and diagonal lines between the relevant note heads.

On pages 56–57 you will find a simple progression on the guitar using minimum movement between chords for a smoother execution and sound.

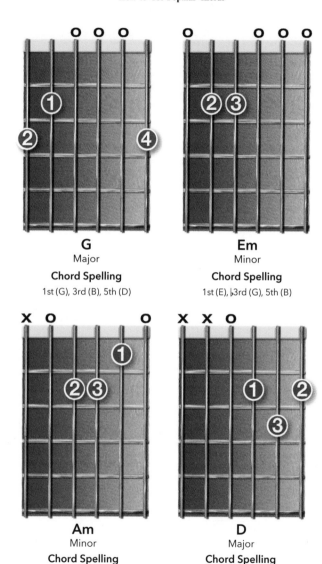

G
Major
Chord Spelling
1st (G), 3rd (B), 5th (D)

Em
Minor
Chord Spelling
1st (E), ♭3rd (G), 5th (B)

Am
Minor
Chord Spelling
1st (A), ♭3rd (C), 5th (E)

D
Major
Chord Spelling
1st (D), 3rd (F♯), 5th (A)

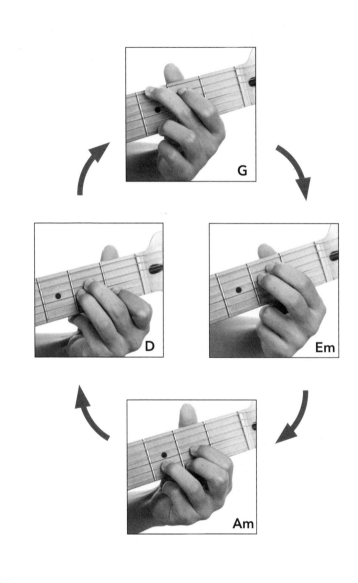

Tips for Smooth Chord Transitions – Piano

One of the best ways to produce smooth chord changes on the piano is to use inversions of the chords. Chords do not have to be played in the strict order they are on the keyboard: often, when moving between chords it's easier to switch the notes so that you don't have to move the whole hand to a new position for each chord. Inversions also help make the combined sound of chords more interesting.

Inversions are normally notated as 'slash' chords:

C/E is 'C major first inversion'
The lowest note of this triad is E, with G and C above it.

C/G is 'C major second inversion'
The lowest note of this triad is G, with C and E above it.

In a chord of 4 or more notes, it's possible for one of the extensions to be the lowest note. For example, 'C major 3rd inversion' uses the 7th as the bass:

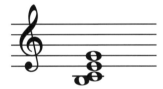

Cmaj7/B is 'C major third inversion'
The lowest note of this chord is B, with C, E and G above it.

Chord Charts

Chord charts are a handy way to communicate information to other players, and are also useful for noting your own chord combinations down.

Simple chord charts are the most common way of notating the chord structure of a song or chord progression. In their most basic form, they include:

- Vertical lines for the start of a new measure
- Chord symbols
- Slash symbols signifying repeat chords

I C / / / I G / / / I

If there is no time signature specified then it's usually safe to assume that the music is in 4/4 time. So for the above you could play the C major chord four times over 4 beats, followed by the G major chord four times over 4 beats.

Rhythm Charts

While standard chord charts are commonly used by pop and rock bands, a chord chart often does not give a clear idea about rhythm. More detailed and complex charts known as 'rhythm charts' are often presented to guitarists involved in recording sessions and those who play in theatre and function band settings.

A typical rhythm chart could be laid out like this:

As a bridge between a chord chart and full-blown musical notation, rhythm charts consist of pitchless notes and rests. The note durations are the same as in regular music notation, so refer back to pages 20–21 if you need a reminder.

Chord Progressions

Chord progressions can take various forms, to the point where they can sound and feel very different from each other, even when using the same chords. Chapters 8 and 9 in this book cover further embellishments and structural techniques that can be used to make a progression sound more interesting, but here is a quick outline of basic differences.

Length

The length of chord progressions can vary, but it's very common for progressions to involve four chords before the sequence repeats. This gives a very comfortable structure for standard timing: four chords, each lasting four beats. A progression can be as long or short as you like though. For example, the ii V I is a popular three-chord progression, and the twelve-bar blues progression is a recognizable longer sequence.

Also worth considering is the frequency of chord changes. On the first beat of each measure gives a strong sense of rhythm, but it's possible to change more or less than that: there can be a chord change every beat, or every two beats, or every two bars, or on the third beat of each measure, and so on.

Major/Minor

The main four progressions in this book take their chords from major scales, as this is the most common and simplest type of scale. Other types of scales can be used too though, as shown on pages 202–203 with minor scales.

Style

The way that chords in a progression are styled can give music its identity. Tips on styling your progressions with melodic and rhythmic techniques can be found in the Writing Songs section.

3

Useful Chord Diagrams

Here you'll find guitar and piano reference
diagrams for major and minor triads in
C, D, E, F, G, A and B, as well as the
dominant 7th, major 7th and minor 7th chords
in these keys. Each chord includes a list of its
notes and a QR code link to the chord online,
where you can hear how it sounds.

C
Major

Chord Spelling
1st (C), 3rd (E), 5th (G)

C
Major

Chord Spelling
1st (C), 3rd (E), 5th (G)

Cm
Minor

X

3

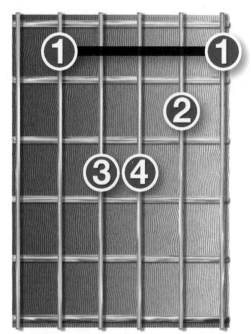

Chord Spelling
1st (C), ♭3rd (E♭), 5th (G)

Cm
Minor

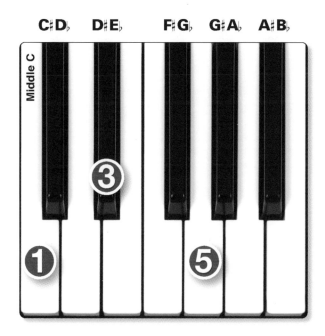

Chord Spelling
1st (C), ♭3rd (E♭), 5th (G)

D
Major

x x o

Chord Spelling
1st (D), 3rd (F♯), 5th (A)

D
Major

Chord Spelling
1st (D), 3rd (F♯), 5th (A)

Dm
Minor

x x o

Chord Spelling
1st (D), ♭3rd (F), 5th (A)

Dm
Minor

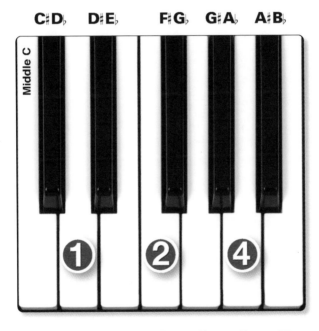

Chord Spelling
1st (D), ♭3rd (F), 5th (A)

E
Major

Chord Spelling
1st (E), 3rd (G♯), 5th (B)

E
Major

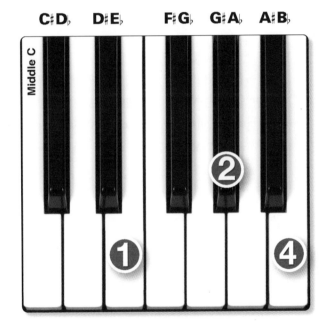

Chord Spelling
1st (E), 3rd (G#), 5th (B)

3

Em
Minor

Chord Spelling
1st (E), ♭3rd (G), 5th (B)

Em
Minor

Chord Spelling
1st (E), ♭3rd (G), 5th (B)

F
Major

Chord Spelling
1st (F), 3rd (A), 5th (C)

F
Major

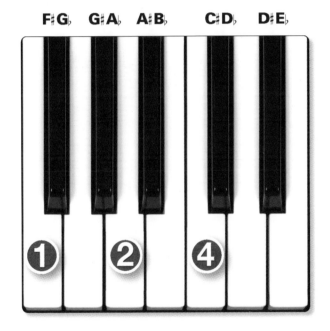

Chord Spelling

1st (F), 3rd (A), 5th (C)

Fm
Minor

Chord Spelling
1st (F), ♭3rd (A♭), 5th (C)

Fm
Minor

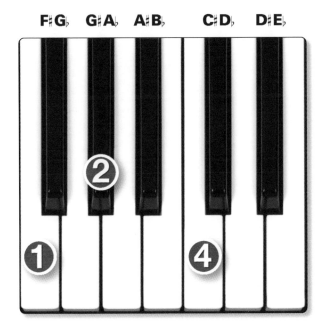

Chord Spelling
1st (F), ♭3rd (A♭), 5th (C)

G
Major

Chord Spelling
1st (G), 3rd (B), 5th (D)

G
Major

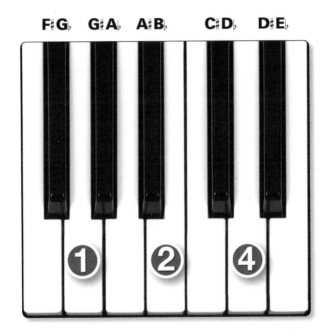

F♯G♭ G♯A♭ A♯B♭ C♯D♭ D♯E♭

F G A B C D E

Chord Spelling
1st (G), 3rd (B), 5th (D)

Gm
Minor

Chord Spelling
1st (G), ♭3rd (B♭), 5th (D)

Gm
Minor

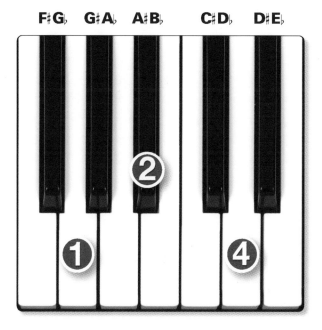

Chord Spelling
1st (G), ♭3rd (B♭), 5th (D)

A
Major

Chord Spelling
1st (A), 3rd (C♯), 5th (E)

A
Major

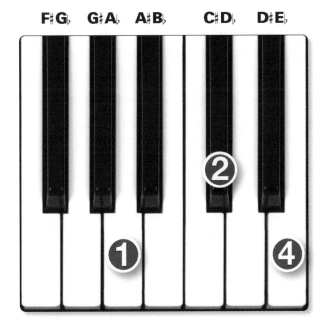

Chord Spelling
1st (A), 3rd (C#), 5th (E)

Am
Minor

Chord Spelling
1st (A), ♭3rd (C), 5th (E)

Am
Minor

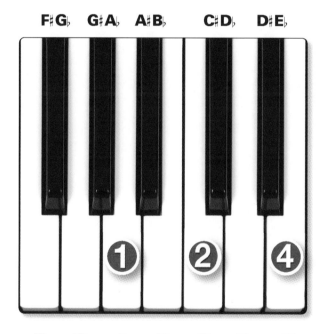

F#G♭ G#A♭ A#B♭   C#D♭ D#E♭

F G A B C D E

Chord Spelling
1st (A), ♭3rd (C), 5th (E)

B
Major

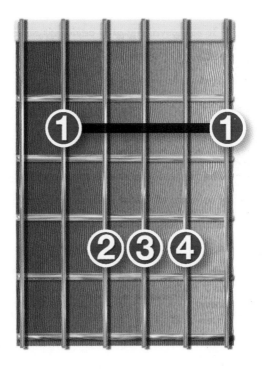

Chord Spelling
1st (B), 3rd (D♯), 5th (F♯)

B
Major

C♯D♭   D♯E♭   F♯G♭   G♯A♭

②   **④**

①

B   C   D   E   F   G   A

Chord Spelling
1st (B), 3rd (D♯), 5th (F♯)

Bm
Minor

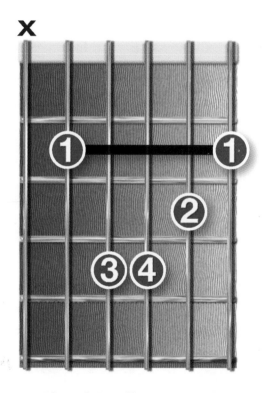

Chord Spelling
1st (B), ♭3rd (D), 5th (F♯)

Bm
Minor

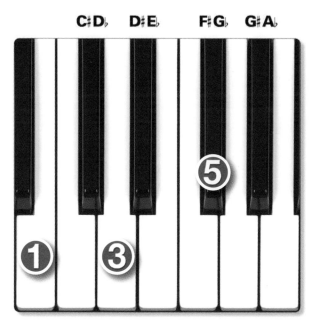

Chord Spelling
1st (B), ♭3rd (D), 5th (F♯)

Dominant 7ths

Seventh chords involve the interval from the first to the seventh note of the scale. For example, in the key of C, this would be the interval from C to B.

There are different types of seventh chords, but dominant 7th chords are especially useful. They are formed by taking the basic major chord and adding the flattened seventh note of the major scale to it.

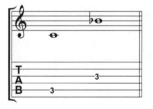

For example, C7 contains the notes: C, E, G, B♭, as shown in the opposite chord diagrams. C7 is called the dominant chord because all the notes it contains fit into the dominant key: all the notes of C7 also appear in the key of G major.

C7
Dominant 7th

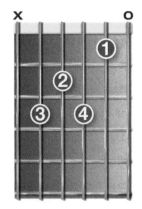

Chord Spelling
1st (C), 3rd (E), 5th (G), ♭7th (B♭)

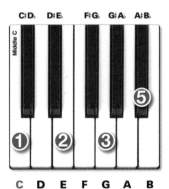

Chord Spelling
1st (C), 3rd (E), 5th (G), ♭7th (B♭)

D7
Dominant 7th

Chord Spelling
1st (D), 3rd (F#), 5th (A), b7th (C)

Chord Spelling
1st (D), 3rd (F#), 5th (A), b7th (C)

E7
Dominant 7th

Chord Spelling
1st (E), 3rd (G#), 5th (B), b7th (D)

E F G A B C D

Chord Spelling
1st (E), 3rd (G#), 5th (B), b7th (D)

F7
Dominant 7th

Chord Spelling
1st (F), 3rd (A), 5th (C), ♭7th (E♭)

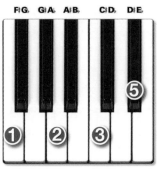

Chord Spelling
1st (F), 3rd (A), 5th (C), ♭7th (E♭)

G7
Dominant 7th

Chord Spelling
1st (G), 3rd (B), 5th (D), ♭7th (F)

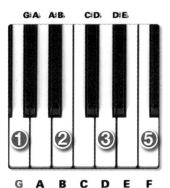

Chord Spelling
1st (G), 3rd (B), 5th (D), ♭7th (F)

A7
Dominant 7th

Chord Spelling
1st (A), 3rd (C♯), 5th (E), ♭7th (G)

Chord Spelling
1st (A), 3rd (C♯), 5th (E), ♭7th (G)

100

B7
Dominant 7th

Chord Spelling
1st (B), 3rd (D♯), 5th (F♯), ♭7th (A)

Chord Spelling
1st (B), 3rd (D♯), 5th (F♯), ♭7th (A)

Major and Minor 7ths

Major 7ths are formed using the seventh note of the major scale.

In C, this would be the interval from C to B. The Cmaj7 chord is therefore produced through the notes C, E, G and B (shown opposite).

If you lower the major seventh interval by a half step it becomes a minor seventh. This interval occurs in both minor 7th and dominant 7th chords. The quality of the 3rd determines whether the chord is a minor 7th or dominant 7th: dominant 7th chords include a major 3rd interval (see earlier), but in minor 7th chords the 3rd is minor too.

The following pages show the major and minor 7th chords for all the main keys, with QR codes that link to the chords on flametreemusic.com.

Cmaj7
Major 7th

Chord Spelling
1st (C), 3rd (E), 5th (G), 7th (B)

Cm7
Minor 7th

Chord Spelling
1st (C), ♭3rd (E♭), 5th (G), ♭7th (B♭)

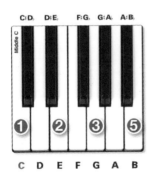

Cmaj7
Major 7th

Chord Spelling
1st (C), 3rd (E), 5th (G), 7th (B)

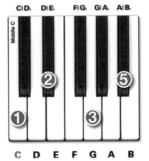

Cm7
Minor 7th

Chord Spelling
1st (C), ♭3rd (E♭), 5th (G), ♭7th (B♭)

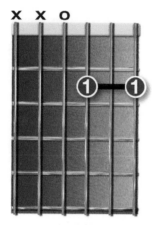

Dmaj7
Major 7th

Chord Spelling
1st (D), 3rd (F#), 5th (A), 7th (C#)

Dm7
Minor 7th

Chord Spelling
1st (D), ♭3rd (F), 5th (A), ♭7th (C)

Dmaj7
Major 7th

Chord Spelling
1st (D), 3rd (F#), 5th (A), 7th (C#)

Dm7
Minor 7th

Chord Spelling
1st (D), ♭3rd (F), 5th (A), ♭7th (C)

Emaj7
Major 7th

Chord Spelling
1st (E), 3rd (G♯), 5th (B), 7th (D♯)

Em7
Minor 7th

Chord Spelling
1st (E), ♭3rd (G), 5th (B), ♭7th (D)

Emaj7
Major 7th

Chord Spelling
1st (E), 3rd (G♯), 5th (B), 7th (D♯)

Em7
Minor 7th

Chord Spelling
1st (E), ♭3rd (G), 5th (B), ♭7th (D)

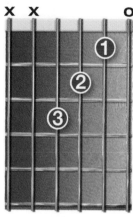

Fmaj7
Major 7th

Chord Spelling
1st (F), 3rd (A), 5th (C), 7th (E)

Fm7
Minor 7th

Chord Spelling
1st (D), ♭3rd (F), 5th (A), ♭7th (C)

Fmaj7
Major 7th

Chord Spelling
1st (F), 3rd (A), 5th (C), 7th (E)

Fm7
Minor 7th

Chord Spelling
1st (F), ♭3rd (A♭), 5th (C), ♭7th (E♭)

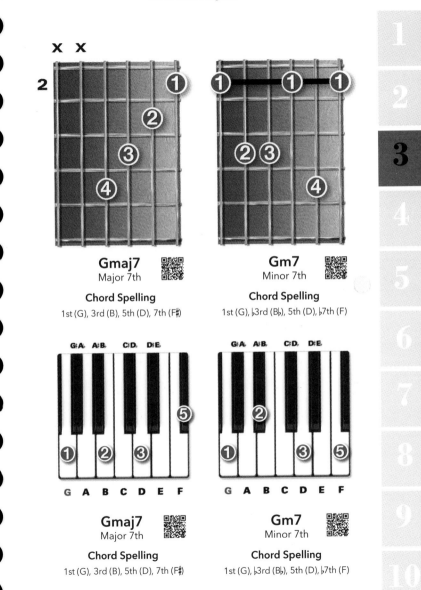

Gmaj7
Major 7th

Chord Spelling
1st (G), 3rd (B), 5th (D), 7th (F♯)

Gm7
Minor 7th

Chord Spelling
1st (G), ♭3rd (B♭), 5th (D), ♭7th (F)

Gmaj7
Major 7th

Chord Spelling
1st (G), 3rd (B), 5th (D), 7th (F♯)

Gm7
Minor 7th

Chord Spelling
1st (G), ♭3rd (B♭), 5th (D), ♭7th (F)

Amaj7
Major 7th

Chord Spelling
1st (A), 3rd (C♯), 5th (E), 7th (G♯)

Am7
Minor 7th

Chord Spelling
1st (A), ♭3rd (C), 5th (E), ♭7th (G)

Amaj7
Major 7th

Chord Spelling
1st (A), 3rd (C♯), 5th (E), 7th (G♯)

Am7
Minor 7th

Chord Spelling
1st (A), ♭3rd (C), 5th (E), ♭7th (G)

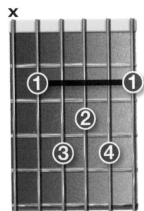

Bmaj7
Major 7th

Chord Spelling
1st (B), 3rd (D#), 5th (F#), 7th (A#)

Bm7
Minor 7th

Chord Spelling
1st (B), ♭3rd (D), 5th (F#), ♭7th (A)

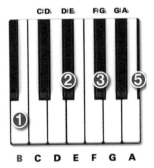

Bmaj7
Major 7th

Chord Spelling
1st (B), 3rd (D#), 5th (F#), 7th (A#)

Bm7
Minor 7th

Chord Spelling
1st (B), ♭3rd (D), 5th (F#), ♭7th (A)

4

Chord Progression:
I V vi IV

This incredibly popular chord progression can
be found in many of the songs heard today.
The following pages will give the chord names
and diagrams for this progression in the keys
of C major, D major, E major, G major and
A major, all with examples of the progression
shown in practice.

The I V vi IV Progression

The I V vi IV progression uses the four chords
indicated by the Roman numerals for whichever key
is chosen. We can work out which chords are needed
using the key's scale. For example, in C major:

C	D	E	F	G	A	B
I	ii	iii	IV	V	vi	vii°

So the chords for this progression in C major are:

C	G	Am	F
I	V	vi	IV
C major	G major	A minor	F major

Opposite you'll see a simple example of this chord
progression shown in practice, and chord diagrams
for the guitar and piano will follow.

Audio example available here:
flametreemusic.com/examples

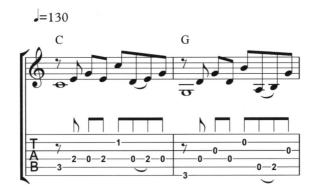

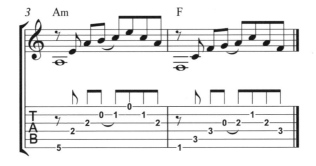

I V vi IV in C: Guitar

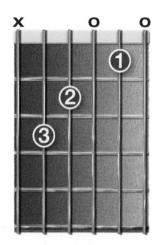

I

C
Major

Chord Spelling
1st (C), 3rd (E), 5th (G)

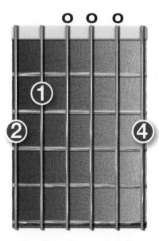

V

G
Major

Chord Spelling
1st (G), 3rd (B), 5th (D)

I V vi IV in C: Guitar

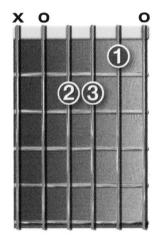

vi

Am
Minor

Chord Spelling
1st (A), ♭3rd (C), 5th (E)

IV

F
Major

Chord Spelling
1st (F), 3rd (A), 5th (C)

I V vi IV in C: Piano

I

C
Major

Chord Spelling
1st (C), 3rd (E), 5th (G)

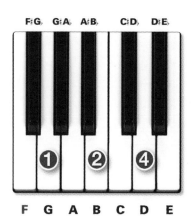

V

G
Major

Chord Spelling
1st (G), 3rd (B), 5th (D)

I V vi IV in C: Piano

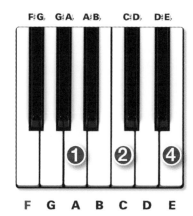

vi

Am
Minor

Chord Spelling
1st (A), ♭3rd (C), 5th (E)

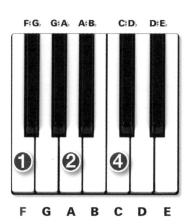

IV

F
Major

Chord Spelling
1st (F), 3rd (A), 5th (C)

Examples:
I V vi IV in C

The following pages demonstrate I V vi IV in action in the key of C.

The first example shows the progression in a different style to the one on page 113. The chord root is played first each time, followed by the rest of the chord with a reggae rhythm later in the bar.

The second example introduces chord inversions: the G chord uses B as its lowest note, allowing a simple step from and to the C note in the first and third bars. The F chord in its second inversion keeps the 'C' prominant, reinforcing the sense of key.

The third example incorporates slight chord variations, adding 7ths to the basic chords while keeping all the notes played within the key of C.

Audio example available here:
flametreemusic.com/examples

♩=120

swung eighth notes, reggae feel: use pick

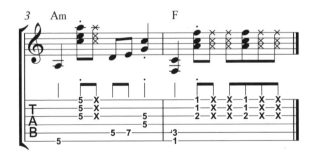

Audio example available here:
flametreemusic.com/examples

Audio example available here:
flametreemusic.com/examples

♩=100

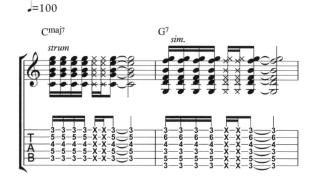

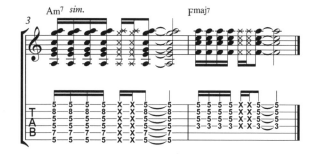

I V vi IV in Other Keys

When chords and chord progressions are described in terms of Roman numerals, they can be applied to any key. Here, using the relevant major scales, we'll show which chords are needed in each of these keys to produce I V vi IV in D major, E major, G major and A major.

D Major: Using the notes of the D major scale...

D	E	F♯	G	A	B	C♯
I	ii	iii	IV	V	vi	vii°

The I V vi IV in D major could be played as:

| D / / / | A / / / | Bm / / / | G / / / |

E Major: Using the notes of the E major scale...

E	F♯	G♯	A	B	C♯	D♯
I	ii	iii	IV	V	vi	vii°

The I V vi IV in E major could be played as...

| E / / / | B / / / | C#m / / / | A / / / |

G Major: Using the notes of the G major scale:

G	A	B	C	D	E	F#
I	ii	iii	IV	V	vi	vii°

The I V vi IV in G major could be played as:

| G / / / | D / / / | Em / / / | C / / / |

A Major: Using the notes of the A major scale...

A	B	C#	D	E	F#	G#
I	ii	iii	IV	V	vi	vii°

The I V vi IV in A major could be played as:

| A / / / | E / / / | F#m / / / | D / / / |

Chord diagrams for these follow, with examples of each shown in practice as a short musical sample.

I V vi IV in D
with Example

As shown on page 122, the chords you would play
for this progression in D are D, A, Bm and G. In
a standard 4/4 song, with four beats per bar, this
could be shown as:

| **D** / / / |
| **A** / / / |
| **Bm** / / / |
| **G** / / / |

The guitar and piano diagrams for these chords follow
on pages 126–129, but first you will see opposite this
progression shown in practice in the key of D. As
with the example in C on page 113, you can see the
chord notes are spread out through the bar in regular
patterns, beginning with the root note each time.

Audio example available here:
flametreemusic.com/examples

♩=130

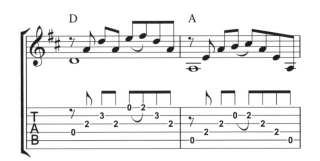

I V vi IV in D: Guitar

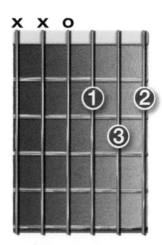

I

D
Major

Chord Spelling
1st (D), 3rd (F#), 5th (A)

V

A
Major

Chord Spelling
1st (A), 3rd (C#), 5th (E)

I V vi IV in D: Guitar

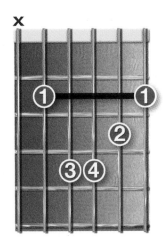

vi

Bm
Minor

Chord Spelling
1st (B), ♭3rd (D), 5th (F♯)

4

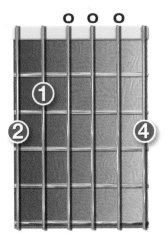

IV

G
Major

Chord Spelling
1st (G), 3rd (B), 5th (D)

I V vi IV in D: Piano

I

D
Major

Chord Spelling
1st (D), 3rd (F♯), 5th (A)

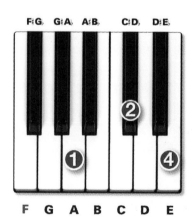

V

A
Major

Chord Spelling
1st (A), 3rd (C♯), 5th (E)

I V vi IV in D: Piano

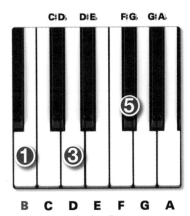

vi

Bm
Minor

Chord Spelling
1st (B), ♭3rd (D), 5th (F♯)

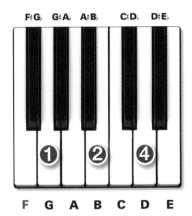

IV

G
Major

Chord Spelling
1st (G), 3rd (B), 5th (D)

I V vi IV in E
with Example

As shown on page 122, the chords you would play for this progression in E are E, B, C#m and A. In a standard 4/4 song, with four beats per bar, this could be shown as:

```
| E  / / / |
| B  / / / |
| C#m / / / |
| A  / / / |
```

Chord diagrams for these follow on pages 132–135, but first you will see opposite this progression shown in practice in the key of E.

Notice how the pattern and rhythm of notes stays the same for each bar. This sets up a satisfying style for each new chord sound that is made.

Audio example available here:
flametreemusic.com/examples

♩=100-160

fingerpicking

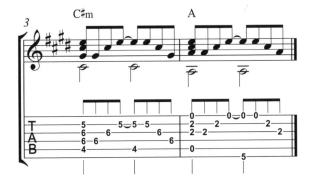

I V vi IV in E: Guitar

I

E
Major

Chord Spelling
1st (E), 3rd (G♯), 5th (B)

V

B
Major

Chord Spelling
1st (B), 3rd (D♯), 5th (F♯)

I V vi IV in E: Guitar

vi

C#m
Minor

Chord Spelling
1st (C#), b3rd (E), 5th (G#)

IV

A
Major

Chord Spelling
1st (A), 3rd (C#), 5th (E)

4

I V vi IV in E: Piano

I

E
Major

Chord Spelling
1st (E), 3rd (G♯), 5th (B)

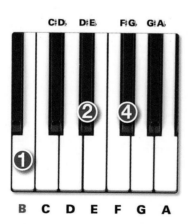

V

B
Major

Chord Spelling
1st (B), 3rd (D♯), 5th (F♯)

I V vi IV in E: Piano

vi

C♯m
Minor

Chord Spelling
1st (C♯), ♭3rd (E), 5th (G♯)

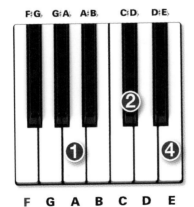

IV

A
Major

Chord Spelling
1st (A), 3rd (C♯), 5th (E)

4

135

I V vi IV in G
with Example

As shown on page 123, the chords you would play for this progression in G are G, D, Em and C. In a standard 4/4 song, with four beats per bar, this could be shown as:

| G / / / |
| D / / / |
| Em / / / |
| C / / / |

Chord diagrams for these follow on pages 138–141, but first you will see opposite this progression shown in practice in the key of G.

The chords here are played first as power chords with the 3rd brought in later in the bar. Notice the rhythm of the first line is echoed in the second.

Audio example available here:
flametreemusic.com/examples

♩=150-175

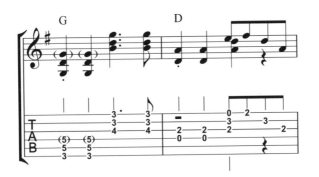

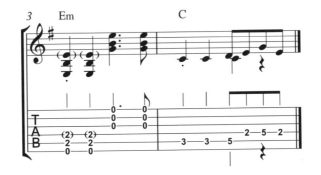

I V vi IV in G: Guitar

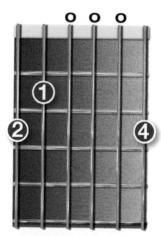

I

G
Major

Chord Spelling
1st (G), 3rd (B), 5th (D)

V

D
Major

Chord Spelling
1st (D), 3rd (F♯), 5th (A)

I V vi IV in G: Guitar

vi

Em
Minor

Chord Spelling
1st (E), ♭3rd (G), 5th (B)

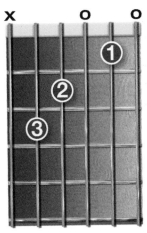

IV

C
Major

Chord Spelling
1st (C), 3rd (E), 5th (G)

I V vi IV in G: Piano

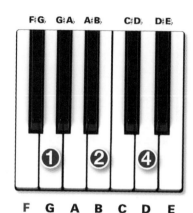

I

G
Major

Chord Spelling
1st (G), 3rd (B), 5th (D)

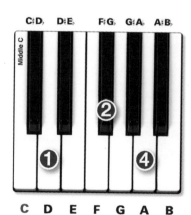

V

D
Major

Chord Spelling
1st (D), 3rd (F#), 5th (A)

I V vi IV in G: Piano

vi

Em
Minor

Chord Spelling
1st (E), b3rd (G), 5th (B)

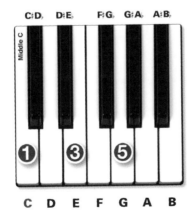

IV

C
Major

Chord Spelling
1st (C), 3rd (E), 5th (G)

I V vi IV in A
with Example

As shown on page 123, the chords you would play for this progression in A are A, E, F#m and D. In a standard 4/4 song, with four beats per bar, this could be shown as:

| A / / / |

| E / / / |

| F#m / / / |

| D / / / |

Chord diagrams for these follow on pages 144–147, but first you will see opposite this progression shown in practice in the key of A. See how the chords are played in full at the start of each bar and followed by notes reinforcing the chord in a regular rhythm. The vi chord is played in its second inversion, with C# in the bass.

Audio example available here:
flametreemusic.com/examples

♩=100-140

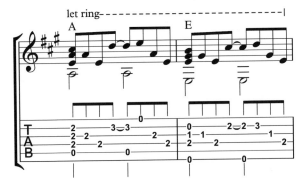

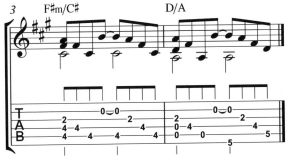

I V vi IV in A: Guitar

I

A
Major

Chord Spelling
1st (A), 3rd (C♯), 5th (E)

V

E
Major

Chord Spelling
1st (E), 3rd (G♯), 5th (B)

I V vi IV in A: Guitar

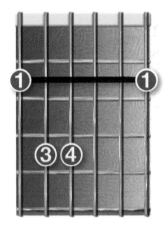

vi

F♯m
Minor

Chord Spelling
1st (F♯), ♭3rd (A), 5th (C♯)

IV

D
Major

Chord Spelling
1st (D), 3rd (F♯), 5th (A)

I V vi IV in A: Piano

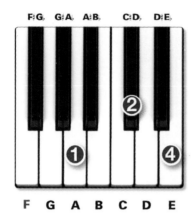

I

A
Major

Chord Spelling
1st (A), 3rd (C♯), 5th (E)

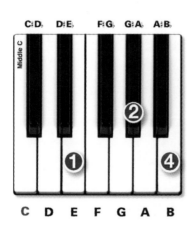

V

E
Major

Chord Spelling
1st (E), 3rd (G♯), 5th (B)

I V vi IV in A: Piano

vi

F♯m
Minor

Chord Spelling
1st (F♯), ♭3rd (A), 5th (C♯)

IV

D
Major

Chord Spelling
1st (D), 3rd (F♯), 5th (A)

147

Variation: vi IV I V

The four chords in the I V vi IV progression can be used in a number of different combinations. Some of the most popular rearrangements of the chords include vi IV I V, and I IV vi V.

Opposite is an example of the vi IV I V variation shown in practice.

It is in the key of C, so we can see how the chords have been taken from the scale of C major:

C	D	E	F	G	A	B
I	ii	iii	IV	V	vi	vii°

Resulting in:

Am	F	C	G
vi	IV	I	V
A minor	F major	C major	G major

Audio example available here:
flametreemusic.com/examples

♩=135

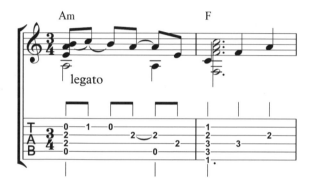

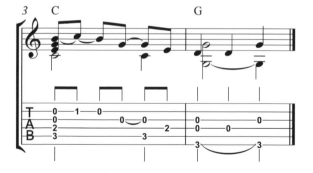

Variation: I IV vi V

This progression is another variation of the same four chords. It switches the position of the IV and V chords, so you can just use the examples shown earlier but taking care to swap those two chords round if you want to try this variation.

Opposite, the example of this progression in action uses the key of G major. We can see which chords were used to form this progression by looking at the scale of G major:

G	A	B	C	D	E	F#
I	ii	iii	IV	V	vi	vii°

So the chords for this progression in G major are:

G	C	Em	D
I	IV	vi	V
G major	C major	E minor	D major

Audio example available here:
flametreemusic.com/examples

♩=120

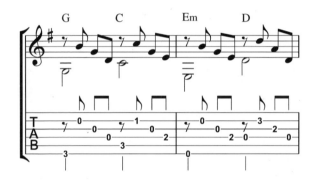

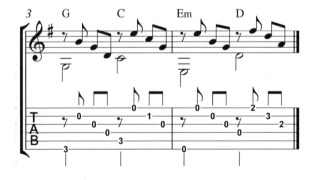

Quick Reference

The I V vi IV progression in the most common keys:

C Major

C	G	Am	F
I	V	vi	IV
1st	5th	6th minor	4th

D Major

D	A	Bm	G
I	V	vi	IV
1st	5th	6th minor	4th

E Major

E	B	C#m	A
I	V	vi	IV
1st	5th	6th minor	4th

G Major

G	D	Em	C
I	V	vi	IV
1st	5th	6th minor	4th

A Major

A	E	F#m	D
I	V	vi	IV
1st	5th	6th minor	4th

5

Chord Progression:
I IV V

Another very common chord progression is the
I IV V. It uses the 'primary chords' of a key, which
are frequently used because of their strong harmonic
links with one another. In Blues music, the same
chord progression is used to great effect with
dominant 7th chords instead of
the basic triads.

The I IV V Progression

As with the previous progression covered in this book, we can work out which chords are needed for the I IV V progression using the key's scale. From the capital Roman numerals, we can see they're all major chords.

For example, in C major:

C	D	E	F	G	A	B
I	ii	iii	IV	V	vi	vii°

The chords we need are:

C	F	G
I	IV	V
C major	F major	G major

The chord diagrams for this progression on both the guitar and piano follow on pages 158–161.

I IV V in C: Guitar

I

C
Major

Chord Spelling
1st (C), 3rd (E), 5th (G)

IV

F
Major

Chord Spelling
1st (F), 3rd (A), 5th (C)

I IV V in C: Guitar

V

G
Major

Chord Spelling
1st (G), 3rd (B), 5th (D)

Presented as a simple chord chart, and assuming
standard 4/4 timing with four beats per bar, this
could be notated as:

| C / / / |
| F / / / |
| G / / / |

I IV V in C: Piano

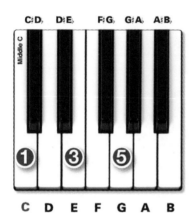

I

C
Major

Chord Spelling
1st (C), 3rd (E), 5th (G)

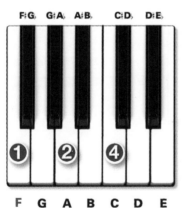

IV

F
Major

Chord Spelling
1st (F), 3rd (A), 5th (C)

I IV V in C: Piano

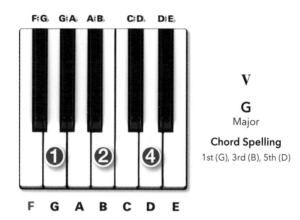

V

G
Major

Chord Spelling
1st (G), 3rd (B), 5th (D)

Presented as a simple chord chart, and assuming standard 4/4 timing with four beats per bar, this could be notated as:

```
|  C  /  /  /  |
|  F  /  /  /  |
|  G  /  /  /  |
```

Examples: I IV V in C

On the right is a simple example of the I IV V progression in C.

There is a use of minims in the bass to establish both the sense of key and the chords themselves. With the I, IV and V notes so prominent in the bass the tonality of C major is confirmed.

The regularity of the rhythm gives the short piece a strong sense of structure while still keeping the sound interesting with the variation in note order for each chord.

This is a straightforward example of the progression in action as all the chords are played very close to each other, and close to the nut on the guitar.

On the next page there is another example of this progression, shown in a different style.

Audio example available here:
flametreemusic.com/examples

♩=140

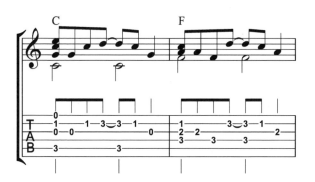

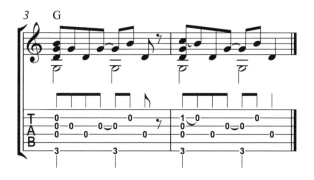

Audio example available here:
flametreemusic.com/examples

♩=140

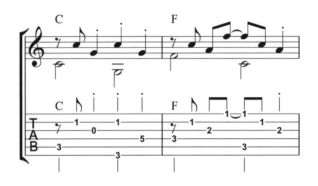

In this example, the C and F chords in the first two bars are reinforced by playing the 1st and 5th of the chords as minims. The crucial 3rd of each chord is part of the rhythmic patterning over these notes.

For the last two bars the notes of the G chord are played largely using open strings, with the low G of the chord plodding as regular minims in the bass while the melody takes the rest of the chord notes and copies the rhythm of the first two bars.

Note the little dot above some of the notes; it means they are to be played 'staccato': distinct or detached from the notes before and after it. This technique helps give the piece a more unique style.

As before, the following pages will demonstrate this progression in the other common keys of D, E, G and A, with examples of each in context plus chord diagrams for the guitar and piano.

IV V in D

with Example

Using the method shown on pages 122–123, this
progression can similarly be transposed to other keys.

To find the progression's chords in D major, we
would look at the notes of the D major scale:

D	E	F#	G	A	B	C#
I	ii	iii	IV	V	vi	vii°

So the chords for this progression in D major are:

D	G	A
I	IV	V
D major	G major	A major

Diagrams for these chords follow on pages 168–171,
but first the sequence is shown in practice opposite.

Audio example available here:
flametreemusic.com/examples

♩=140

Strummed acoustic or rock electric

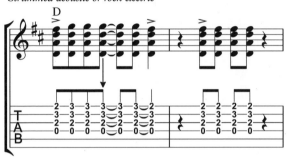

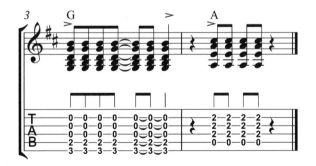

I IV V in D: Guitar

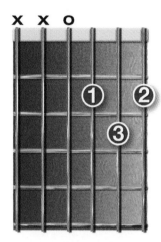

I

D
Major

Chord Spelling
1st (D), 3rd (F♯), 5th (A)

IV

G
Major

Chord Spelling
1st (G), 3rd (B), 5th (D)

I IV V in D: Guitar

V

A
Major

Chord Spelling
1st (A), 3rd (C♯), 5th (E)

Presented as a simple chord chart, and assuming standard 4/4 timing with four beats per bar, this could be notated as:

| D / / / |
| G / / / |
| A / / / |

I IV V in D: Piano

I

D
Major

Chord Spelling
1st (D), 3rd (F♯), 5th (A)

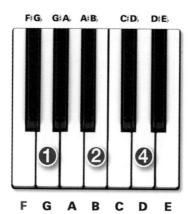

IV

G
Major

Chord Spelling
1st (G), 3rd (B), 5th (D)

I IV V in D: Piano

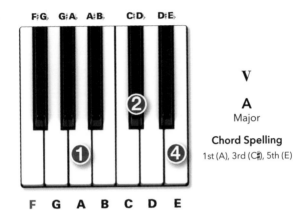

V

A
Major

Chord Spelling
1st (A), 3rd (C♯), 5th (E)

Presented as a simple chord chart, and assuming standard 4/4 timing with four beats per bar, this could be notated as:

| D / / / |
| G / / / |
| A / / / |

I IV V in E
with Example

To find the progression's chords in E major, we would look at the notes of the E major scale:

E	F♯	G♯	A	B	C♯	D♯
I	ii	iii	IV	V	vi	vii°

So the chords for this progression in E major are:

E	A	B
I	IV	V
E major	A major	B major

Diagrams for these chords follow on pages 174–177, and the opposite example shows them in use. The 'P.M' instruction for the guitar means 'palm mute', where the strumming hand is pressed lightly on the strings while still allowing them to sound.

Audio example available here:
flametreemusic.com/examples

♩=100-120

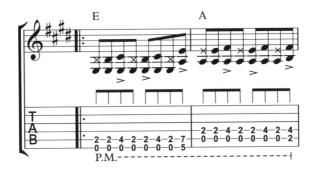

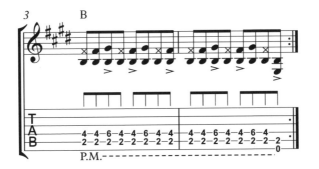

I IV V in E: Guitar

I

E
Major

Chord Spelling
1st (E), 3rd (G♯), 5th (B)

IV

A
Major

Chord Spelling
1st (A), 3rd (C♯), 5th (E)

I IV V in E: Guitar

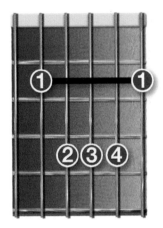

V

B
Major

Chord Spelling
1st (B), 3rd (D♯), 5th (F♯)

Presented as a simple chord chart, and assuming standard 4/4 timing with four beats per bar, this could be notated as:

```
| E / / / |
| A / / / |
| B / / / |
```

I IV V in E: Piano

I

E
Major

Chord Spelling
1st (E), 3rd (G♯), 5th (B)

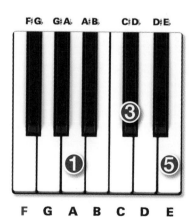

IV

A
Major

Chord Spelling
1st (A), 3rd (C♯), 5th (E)

I IV V in E: Piano

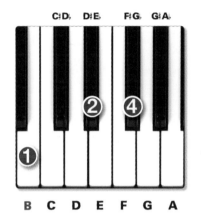

V

B
Major

Chord Spelling
1st (B), 3rd (D♯), 5th (F♯)

Presented as a simple chord chart, and assuming standard 4/4 timing with four beats per bar, this could be notated as:

| E / / / |
| A / / / |
| B / / / |

I IV V in G with Example

To find the progression's chords in G major, we would look at the notes of the G major scale:

G	A	B	C	D	E	F♯
I	ii	iii	IV	V	vi	vii°

So the chords for this progression in G major are:

G	C	D
I	IV	V
G major	C major	D major

Diagrams for these chords follow on pages 180–183, but first you will see opposite this progression shown in practice in the key of G.

Audio example available here:
flametreemusic.com/examples

♩=180-200

strummed

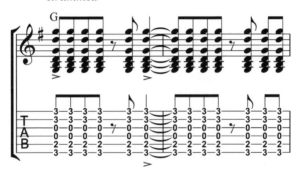

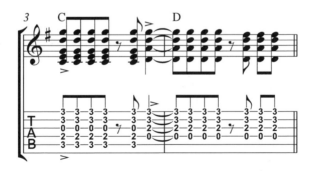

I IV V in G: Guitar

I

G
Major

Chord Spelling
1st (G), 3rd (B), 5th (D)

IV

C
Major

Chord Spelling
1st (C), 3rd (E), 5th (G)

IV V in G: Guitar

X X O

V

D
Major

Chord Spelling
1st (D), 3rd (F♯), 5th (A)

Presented as a simple chord chart, and assuming standard 4/4 timing with four beats per bar, this could be notated as:

```
| G / / / |
| C / / / |
| D / / / |
```

181

I IV V in G: Piano

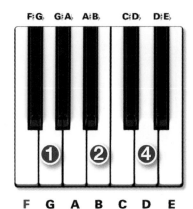

F♯G♭ G♯A♭ A♯B♭   C♯D♭ D♯E♭

I

G
Major

Chord Spelling
1st (G), 3rd (B), 5th (D)

① **②** **④**

F G A B C D E

C♯D♭ D♯E♭   F♯G♭ G♯A♭ A♯B♭

Middle C

IV

C
Major

Chord Spelling
1st (C), 3rd (E), 5th (G)

① **③** **⑤**

C D E F G A B

I IV V in G: Piano

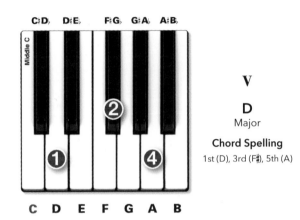

V

D

Major

Chord Spelling

1st (D), 3rd (F♯), 5th (A)

Presented as a simple chord chart, and assuming standard 4/4 timing with four beats per bar, this could be notated as:

| **G** / / / |

| **C** / / / |

| **D** / / / |

I IV V in A
with Example

To find the progression's chords in A major, we would look at the notes of the A major scale:

A	B	C♯	D	E	F♯	G♯
I	ii	iii	IV	V	vi	vii°

So the chords for this progression in A major are:

A	D	E
I	IV	V
A major	D major	E major

Diagrams for these chords follow on pages 186–189, but first you will see opposite this progression shown in practice in the key of A.

Audio example available here:
flametreemusic.com/examples

♩=150-180

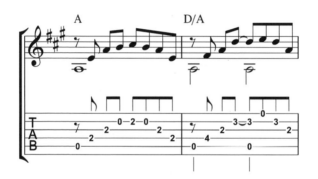

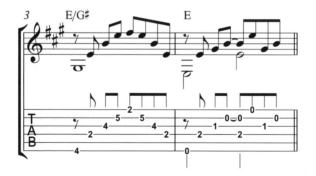

I IV V in A: Guitar

I

A
Major

Chord Spelling
1st (A), 3rd (C♯), 5th (E)

IV

D
Major

Chord Spelling
1st (D), 3rd (F♯), 5th (A)

I IV V in A: Guitar

V

E
Major

Chord Spelling
1st (E), 3rd (G♯), 5th (B)

Presented as a simple chord chart, and assuming standard 4/4 timing with four beats per bar, this could be notated as:

| **A** / / / |
| **D** / / / |
| **E** / / / |

I IV V in A: Piano

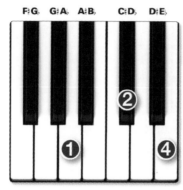

I

A
Major

Chord Spelling
1st (A), 3rd (C♯), 5th (E)

IV

D
Major

Chord Spelling
1st (D), 3rd (F♯), 5th (A)

I IV V in A: Piano

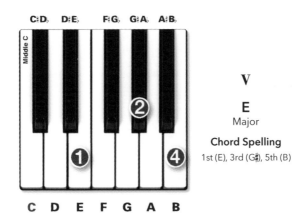

V

E
Major

Chord Spelling
1st (E), 3rd (G♯), 5th (B)

Presented as a simple chord chart, and assuming standard 4/4 timing with four beats per bar, this could be notated as:

| A / / / |

| D / / / |

| E / / / |

Variations

Some types of variations of the I IV V progression can include simple differences in style or rhythm, the rearrangement or extension of existing chords in the sequence, or the addition of 7th chords.

Opposite is an example in A major that plays with the movement of chord changes. It keeps a consistent quaver patterning of notes but switches chords more frequently than once per bar: the first two bars cover four chords (I IV V IV) and repeats those chords in bars 3 and 4, but using a dominant 7th in place of the regular V chord.

On page 194 is an example that adds 7ths to all of the chords used, explained in more detail on pages 192–193.

On pages 199–201 is an example of a twelve-bar blues sequence, a longer version of the I IV V.

Audio example available here:
flametreemusic.com/examples

♩=140-160

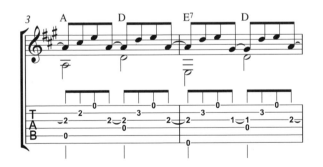

Variation: Adding 7ths

A straightforward popular version of the I IV V progression using 7ths would be for all three chords to be in their dominant 7th forms. A dominant 7th chord uses the same major triad, but with an added flattened 7th.

As we already know the chords for I IV V in C major, we can use their relevant scales to find the 'seventh' note for C, F, and G:

C	D	E	F	G	A	B
F	G	A	B♭	C	D	E
G	A	B	C	D	E	F♯
I	ii	iii	IV	V	vi	vii°

So adding a flattened 7th to each of the chords gives us:

| I | = | C | (C, E, G) |

with added ♭7 becomes:

| I7 | = | C7 | (C, E, G, B♭) |

| IV | = | F | (F, A, C) |

with added ♭7 becomes:

| IV7 | = | F7 | (F, A, C, E♭) |

| V | = | G | (G, B, D) |

with added ♭7 becomes:

| V7 | = | G7 | (G, B, D, F) |

V7 chords in particular are very popular in blues music.

On the next page you'll find an example of this chord sequence of dominant 7th chords, applied to the key of E major.

$\quad\downarrow=150$

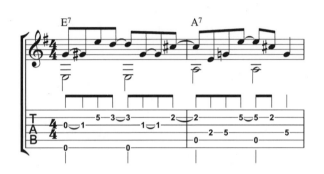

The example opposite demonstrates the I7 IV7 V7 sequence in the context of E major.

To find the seventh note for the chords in E major we can look at the relevant scales:

E	F♯	G♯	A	B	C♯	D♯
A	B	C♯	D	E	F♯	G♯
B	C♯	D♯	E	F♯	G♯	A♯
I	ii	iii	IV	V	vi	vii°

So adding flattened 7ths to the triads gives:

I7	=	E7	(E, G♯, B, D)
IV7	=	A7	(A, C♯, E, G)
V7	=	B7	(B, D♯, F♯, A)

Chord diagrams follow on the next two pages for the guitar and piano, showing the chords used in the opposite example.

I7

E7
Dominant 7th

Chord Spelling
1st (E), 3rd (G♯), 5th (B), ♭7th (D)

IV7

B7
Dominant 7th

Chord Spelling
1st (B), 3rd (D♯), 5th (F♯), ♭7th (A)

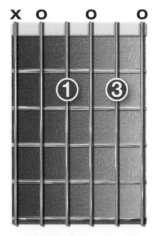

V7

A7
Dominant 7th

Chord Spelling
1st (A), 3rd (C♯), 5th (E), ♭7th (G)

196

I7

E7
Dominant 7th

Chord Spelling
1st (E), 3rd (G♯), 5th (B), ♭7th (D)

IV7

B7
Dominant 7th

Chord Spelling
1st (B), 3rd (D♯), 5th (F♯), ♭7th (A)

V7

A7
Dominant 7th

Chord Spelling
1st (A), 3rd (C♯), 5th (E), ♭7th (G)

Variation:

The Twelve-Bar Blues

Perhaps most famously, the I IV V progression forms the basis of the twelve-bar blues. This can take various forms, with a typical example being:

I	I	I	I
IV	IV	I	I
V	IV	I	I

The chord diagrams for these would be the same as the ones covered earlier in this chapter.

It's common to use 7ths here too, so play around with I7, IV7 and V7 variants to get the effect you want.

Over the next 3 pages this progression is shown in the key of E, using dominant 7ths for the final V and IV chords.

Audio example available here:
flametreemusic.com/examples

♩=80-100, *light swing*

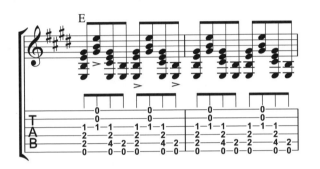

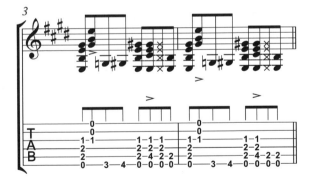

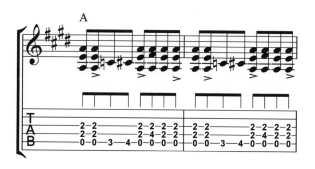

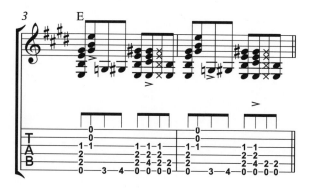

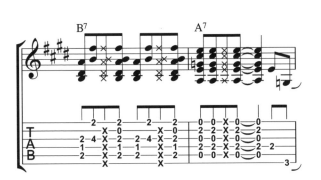

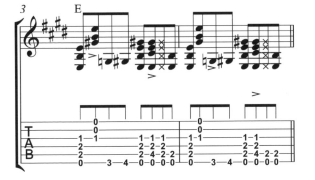

Using the Minor Scale:

i iv V

While there is only one major scale, there are three types of minor scale: the natural minor scale, the harmonic minor scale, and the melodic minor scale.

Progressions using minor scales often borrow from other minor scales dependent on which notes they offer. The harmonic minor scale is useful, as the flattened 7th note allows a V7 chord to be formed. It differs from its major form with a flattened 3rd and a flattened 6th. Seen together:

A Major

A	B	C♯	D	E	F♯	G♯

A Minor Harmonic

A	B	C	D	E	F	G♯

We can see how the minor scale notes harmonize:

A	B	C	D	E	F	G#
i	ii°	III+	iv	V	VI	vii°
Am	B°	C+	Dm	E	F	G#°
Minor	Diminished	Augmented	Minor	Major	Major	Diminished

The harmonized scale gives us the chords that fit within this key:

i:	Am	(A, C, E)
ii°:	B°	(B, D, F)
III+:	C+	(C, E, G#)
iv:	Dm	(D, F, A)
V:	E	(E, G#, B)
VI:	F	(F, A, C)
vii°:	G#°	(G#, B, D)

As the relative minor (see page 344–345) of C major, A minor comes in handy. Other useful minor keys include: E minor, D minor and B minor, as these are common and relatively easy to play in.

The example opposite shows this progression in action using E minor harmonic as its basis. We can understand the chords used by looking at this scale:

E	F#	G	A	B	C	D#
i	ii°	III+	iv	V	VI	vii°

So the chords for this harmonic minor progression in E minor are:

Em	Am	B
i	iv	V
E minor	A minor	B major

Using the scale to find the basic triad notes:

E minor:	E, G, B
A minor:	A, C, E
B major:	B, D#, F#

The example opposite incorporates a dominant 7th chord for the V (B major). Chord diagrams for both guitar and piano follow.

Audio example available here:
flametreemusic.com/examples

$\stackrel{\downarrow}{=}150$

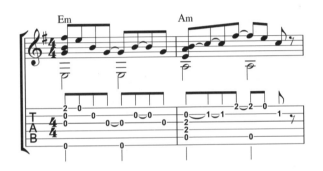

i

Em
Minor

Chord Spelling
1st (E), ♭3rd (G), 5th (B)

iv

Am
Minor

Chord Spelling
1st (A), ♭3rd (C), 5th (E)

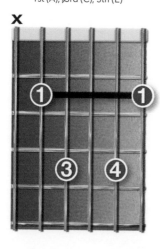

V7

B7
Dominant 7th

Chord Spelling
1st (B), 3rd (D♯), 5th (F♯), ♭7th (A)

i

Em
Minor

Chord Spelling
1st (E), ♭3rd (G), 5th (B)

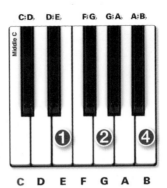

iv

Am
Minor

Chord Spelling
1st (A), ♭3rd (C), 5th (E)

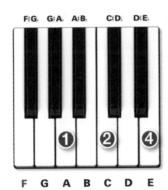

V7

B7
Dominant 7th

Chord Spelling
1st (B), 3rd (D♯), 5th (F♯), ♭7th (A)

207

Quick Reference

The I IV V progression in the most common keys:

C Major

C	F	G
I	IV	V
1st	4th	5th

D Major

D	G	A
I	IV	V
1st	4th	5th

E Major

E	A	B
I	IV	V
1st	4th	5th

G Major

G	C	D
I	IV	V
1st	4th	5th

A Major

A	D	E
I	IV	V
1st	4th	5th

6

Chord Progression:
ii V I

The third main chord progression you're likely to
come across in lots of music is the ii V I. A popular
feature in Jazz music, this three-chord progression
contains the satisfying V to I chord movement,
which feels natural and pleasing to the ear,
especially at the end of a section.

The ii V I Progression

As with the previous progression covered in this book, we can work out which chords are needed for the ii V I progression using the key's scale.

For example, in C major:

C	D	E	F	G	A	B
I	ii	iii	IV	V	vi	vii°

The chords we need are:

Dm	G	C
ii	V	I
D minor	G major	C major

The chord diagrams for this progression in C on both the guitar and piano will follow on the next few pages, followed by some examples showing the progression in action.

ii V I in C: Guitar

ii

Dm
Minor

Chord Spelling
1st (D), ♭3rd (F), 5th (A)

V

G
Major

Chord Spelling
1st (G), 3rd (B), 5th (D)

ii V I in C: Guitar

I

C
Major

Chord Spelling
1st (C), 3rd (E), 5th (G)

Presented as a simple chord chart, and assuming standard 4/4 timing with four beats per bar, this could be notated as:

| Dm / / / |
| G / / / |
| C / / / |

ii V I in C: Piano

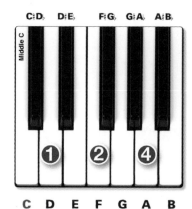

ii

Dm
Minor

Chord Spelling
1st (D), ♭3rd (F), 5th (A)

V

G
Major

Chord Spelling
1st (G), 3rd (B), 5th (D)

ii V I in C: Piano

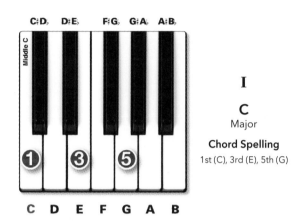

I

C
Major

Chord Spelling
1st (C), 3rd (E), 5th (G)

6

Presented as a simple chord chart, and assuming
standard 4/4 timing with four beats per bar, this
could be notated as:

| Dm / / / |
| G / / / |
| C / / / |

Examples: ii V I in C

On the right is a simple example of the ii V I progression in C.

As a relatively straightforward piece to play, it uses quick quaver notes and arpeggio-like structures (see page 360) to decorate the root note of the chord, which remains played in the bass.

On page 220 there is another example of the ii V I progression in C, demonstrating how a change in rhythm or chord playing style can transform the effect of the chords played. There, the chords are played as solid minim blocks, with chord inversions used to vary the sound.

While that the chord types still change once per bar, the second half of each bar inverts the bar's chord to give a similar but distinct sound.

Audio example available here:
flametreemusic.com/examples

♩=110

let ring throughout

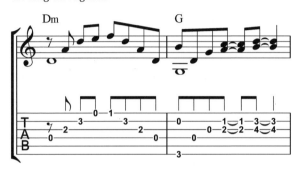

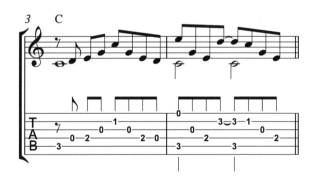

Audio example available here:
flametreemusic.com/examples

♩=100

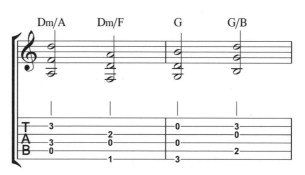

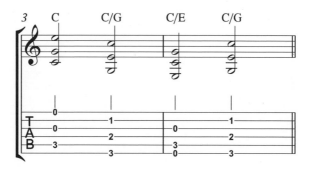

ii V I in D with Example

To find the progression's chords in D major, we would look at the notes of the D major scale:

D	E	F♯	G	A	B	C♯
I	ii	iii	IV	V	vi	vii°

So the chords for this progression in D major are:

Em	G	A
ii	V	I
E minor	A major	D major

Diagrams for these chords on both guitar and piano follow on pages 224–227.

Opposite you can see this progression shown in practice in the key of D.

Audio example available here:
flametreemusic.com/examples

♩=100-120

let ring throughout

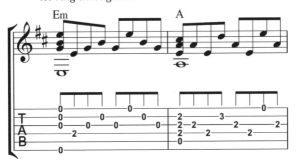

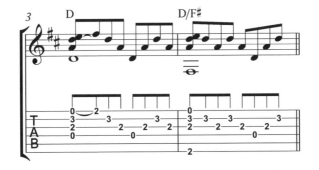

ii V I in D: Guitar

ii

Em
Minor

Chord Spelling
1st (E), ♭3rd (G), 5th (B)

V

A
Major

Chord Spelling
1st (A), 3rd (C♯), 5th (E)

ii V I in D: Guitar

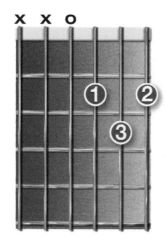

I

D
Major

Chord Spelling
1st (D), 3rd (F♯), 5th (A)

Presented as a simple chord chart, and assuming
standard 4/4 timing with four beats per bar, this
could be notated as:

| Em / / / |
| A / / / |
| D / / / |

ii V I in D: Piano

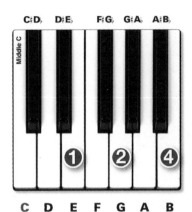

ii

Em
Minor

Chord Spelling
1st (E), ♭3rd (G), 5th (B)

V

A
Major

Chord Spelling
1st (A), 3rd (C♯), 5th (E)

ii V I in D: Piano

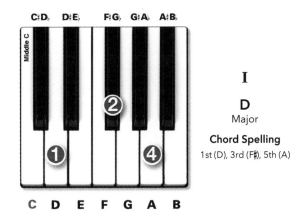

I

D
Major

Chord Spelling
1st (D), 3rd (F♯), 5th (A)

Presented as a simple chord chart, and assuming standard 4/4 timing with four beats per bar, this could be notated as:

| **Em** / / / |
| **A** / / / |
| **D** / / / |

227

ii V I in E
with Example

To find the progression's chords in E major, we would look at the notes of the E major scale:

E	F♯	G♯	A	B	C♯	D♯
I	ii	iii	IV	V	vi	vii°

So the chords for this progression in E major are:

F♯m	B	E
ii	V	I
F♯ minor	B major	E major

Diagrams for these chords for the guitar and piano follow on pages 230–233, but first you will see opposite this progression shown in practice in the key of E. It ends on a 6th chord; you can find out more about those on pages 328–329.

Audio example available here:
flametreemusic.com/examples

♩=100-120

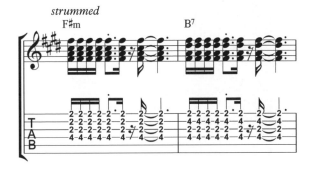

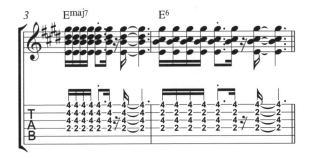

ii V I in E: Guitar

ii

F♯m
Minor

Chord Spelling
1st (F♯), ♭3rd (A), 5th (C♯)

V

B
Major

Chord Spelling
1st (B), 3rd (D♯), 5th (F♯)

ii V I in E: Guitar

I

E
Major

Chord Spelling
1st (E), 3rd (G♯), 5th (B)

Presented as a simple chord chart, and assuming standard 4/4 timing with four beats per bar, this could be notated as:

| F♯m / / / |
| B / / / |
| E / / / |

ii V I in E: Piano

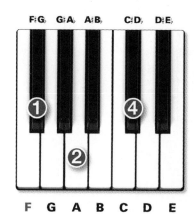

ii

F#m
Minor

Chord Spelling
1st (F#), ♭3rd (A), 5th (C#)

V

B
Major

Chord Spelling
1st (B), 3rd (D#), 5th (F#)

232

ii V I in E: Piano

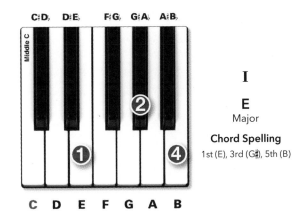

I

E
Major

Chord Spelling
1st (E), 3rd (G♯), 5th (B)

Presented as a simple chord chart, and assuming standard 4/4 timing with four beats per bar, this could be notated as:

| F♯m / / / |
| B / / / |
| E / / / |

233

ii V I in G
with Example

To find the progression's chords in G major, we would look at the notes of the G major scale:

G	A	B	C	D	E	F♯
I	ii	iii	IV	V	vi	vii°

So the chords for this progression in G major are:

Am	D	G
ii	V	I
A minor	D major	G major

Diagrams for these chords follow on pages 236–239, but first you will see opposite this progression shown in practice in the key of G. For more on sus chords, 'add 9' and 6ths, see the Chord Embellishments section (Chapter 8).

Audio example available here:
flametreemusic.com/examples

♩=90-100

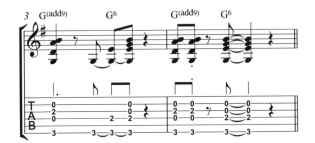

ii V I in G: Guitar

ii

Am
Minor

Chord Spelling
1st (A), ♭3rd (C), 5th (E)

V

D
Major

Chord Spelling
1st (D), 3rd (F♯), 5th (A)

ii V I in G: Guitar

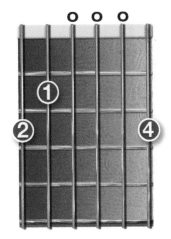

I

G
Major

Chord Spelling
1st (G), 3rd (B), 5th (D)

Presented as a simple chord chart, and assuming standard 4/4 timing with four beats per bar, this could be notated as:

| Am / / / |
| D / / / |
| G / / / |

ii V I in G: Piano

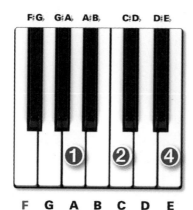

ii

Am
Minor

Chord Spelling
1st (A), ♭3rd (C), 5th (E)

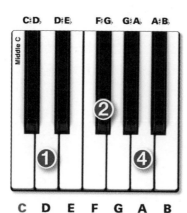

V

D
Major

Chord Spelling
1st (D), 3rd (F♯), 5th (A)

ii V I in G: Piano

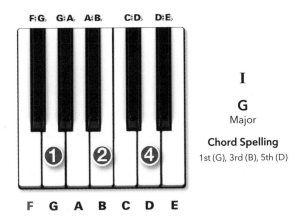

I

G
Major

Chord Spelling
1st (G), 3rd (B), 5th (D)

Presented as a simple chord chart, and assuming standard 4/4 timing with four beats per bar, this could be notated as:

| Am / / / |
| D / / / |
| G / / / |

ii V I in A
with Example

To find the progression's chords in A major, we would look at the notes of the A major scale:

A	B	C#	D	E	F#	G#
I	ii	iii	IV	V	vi	vii°

So the chords for this progression in A major are:

Bm	E	A
ii	V	I
B minor	E major	A major

Diagrams for these chords follow on pages 242–245, but first you will see opposite this progression shown in practice in the key of A. Again, for more on 'add 9' and sus chords, see the Chord Embellishments section in Chapter 8.

Audio example available here: flametreemusic.com/examples

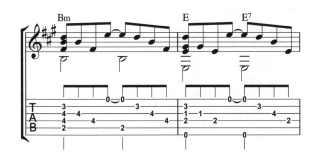

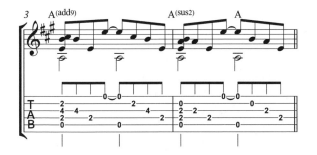

ii V I in A: Guitar

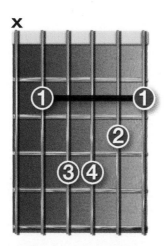

ii

Bm
Minor

Chord Spelling
1st (B), ♭3rd (D), 5th (F♯)

V

E
Major

Chord Spelling
1st (E), 3rd (G♯), 5th (B)

ii V I in A: Guitar

I

A
Major

Chord Spelling
1st (A), 3rd (C♯), 5th (E)

Presented as a simple chord chart, and assuming standard 4/4 timing with four beats per bar, this could be notated as:

| Bm / / / |
| E / / / |
| A / / / |

243

ii V I in A: Piano

ii

Bm
Minor

Chord Spelling
1st (B), ♭3rd (D), 5th (F♯)

V

E
Major

Chord Spelling
1st (E), 3rd (G♯), 5th (B)

244

ii V I in A: Piano

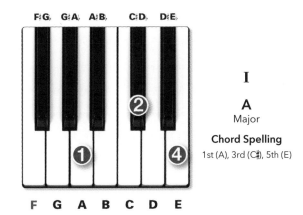

I

A
Major

Chord Spelling
1st (A), 3rd (C♯), 5th (E)

6

Presented as a simple chord chart, and assuming standard 4/4 timing with four beats per bar, this could be notated as:

| Bm / / / |
| E / / / |
| A / / / |

245

Variations

Some types of variations of the standard ii V I
sequence include altering the rhythmic style, adding
7ths, or adding in other chords. You may wish, for
example, to lengthen the ii V I into a four-chord
setup by beginning the progression with the I chord.

Opposite is an example of the ii V I progression
in C using chord inversions, 7ths, and a simple
rhythmic structure. Notice how the bass notes
barely vary: the chord notes come through in the
movement of the melody.

On page 248 is an example of the ii V I sequence
using 7ths. In each bar, the dotted note makes
the longer following note feel offset from the main
beat (it begins halfway through the second beat of
the bar), giving it that 'swing or shuffle feel' and
offering a different sound to the same basic chords.

Audio example available here:
flametreemusic.com/examples

♩=70-80

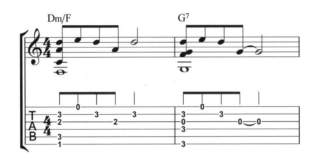

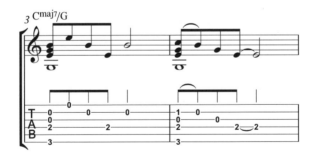

Audio example available here:
flametreemusic.com/examples

♩=120

swing or shuffle feel

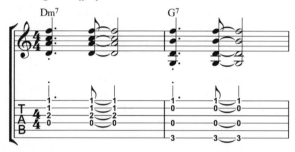

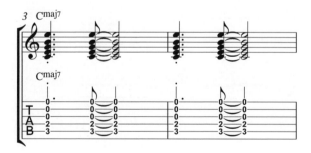

Variation: Adding 7ths

A popular use of the progression would include adding 7ths. The example opposite uses a ii7 V7 Imaj7 progression. This includes the three different types of 7th chords: dominant 7ths, major 7ths and minor 7ths.

To find the 'seventh' note for Dm, G and C, we can take the notes from the relevant major scales, and adjust the 3rds and 7ths as necessary:

ii7	=	Dm7 (D, F, A, C)
V7	=	G7 (G, B, D, F)
Imaj7	=	Cmaj7 (C, E, G, B)

Chord diagrams for these follow on pages 252–253.

In the opposite example, the G7 chord has been extended to become G13, and inversions are used in the first and third bar.

Audio example available here:
flametreemusic.com/examples

♩=120

bossa nova

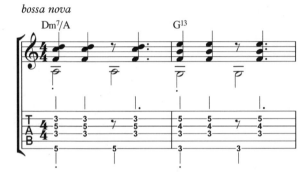

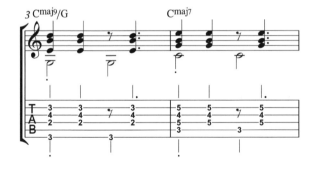

ii7

Dm7
Minor 7th

Chord Spelling
1st (D), ♭3rd (F), 5th (A), ♭7th (C)

V7

G7
Dominant 7th

Chord Spelling
1st (G), 3rd (B), 5th (D), ♭7th (F)

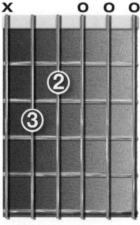

Imaj7

Cmaj7
Major 7th

Chord Spelling
1st (C), 3rd (E), 5th (G), 7th (B)

ii7

Dm7
Minor 7th

Chord Spelling
1st (D), ♭3rd (F), 5th (A), ♭7th (C)

V7

G7
Dominant 7th

Chord Spelling
1st (G), 3rd (B), 5th (D), ♭7th (F)

Imaj7

Cmaj7
Major 7th

Chord Spelling
1st (C), 3rd (E), 5th (G), 7th (B)

253

Using the Minor Scale: ii V i

Like the minor i iv V (see pages 202–207), we can use a minor harmonic scale for this progression. The example opposite in E minor uses the chords:

F#°	B	Em
ii°	V	i
F# diminished	B major	E minor

As in the example opposite, 7ths are often added to the ii° and V chords, to give:

F#ø:	F#	A	C	E
and B7:	B	D#	F#	A

Half-diminished (ø) chords are sometimes notated as 'm7♭5', as they're made up of minor 3rd, lowered 5th and minor 7th intervals. Relevant chord diagrams for this sequence are on the next pages.

Audio example available here:
flametreemusic.com/examples

♩=100

let ring throughout

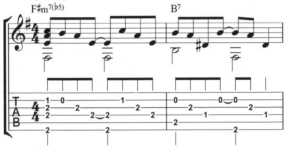

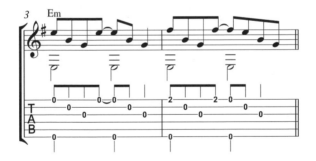

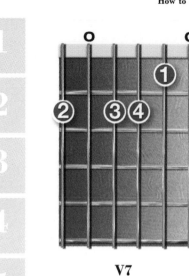

F♯m7♭5
Minor 7th Flattened 5th

Chord Spelling
1st (F♯), ♭3rd (A), ♭5th (C), ♭7th (E)

V7

B7
Dominant 7th

Chord Spelling
1st (B), 3rd (D♯), 5th (F♯), ♭7th (A)

i

Em
Minor

Chord Spelling
1st (E), ♭3rd (G), 5th (B)

F♯m7♭5
Minor 7th Flattened 5th

Chord Spelling
1st (F♯), ♭3rd (A), ♭5th (C), ♭7th (E)

V7

B7
Dominant 7th

Chord Spelling
1st (B), 3rd (D♯), 5th (F♯), ♭7th (A)

i

Em
Minor

Chord Spelling
1st (E), ♭3rd (G), 5th (B)

Quick Reference

The ii V I progression in the most common keys:

C Major

Dm	G	C
ii	V	I
minor 2nd	5th	1st

D Major

Em	A	D
ii	V	I
minor 2nd	5th	1st

E Major

F#m	B	E
ii	V	I
minor 2nd	5th	1st

G Major

Am	D	G
ii	V	I
minor 2nd	5th	1st

A Major

Bm	E	A
ii	V	I
minor 2nd	5th	1st

7

Chord Progression: I vi IV V

The final main chord progression focused on in
detail in this book is actually a variation of the
I V vi IV progression. This is a different
ordering of the same four chords that
was immensely popular in the 20th century,
and which is now often referred to as the ''50s'
chord progression.

The I vi IV V Progression

In C major, the chords needed for the I vi IV V progression are formed using the notes of the C major scale:

C	D	E	F	G	A	B
I	ii	iii	IV	V	vi	vii°

So the chords for this progression in C major are:

C	Am	F	G
I	vi	IV	V
C major	A minor	F major	G major

The following pages show the chord diagrams for this progression in C for the guitar and piano, followed by some simple examples of the progression in practice.

I vi IV V in C: Guitar

I

C
Major

Chord Spelling
1st (C), 3rd (E), 5th (G)

vi

Am
Minor

Chord Spelling
1st (A), ♭3rd (C), 5th (E)

I vi IV V in C: Guitar

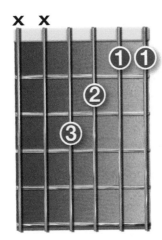

IV

F
Major

Chord Spelling
1st (F), 3rd (A), 5th (C)

V

G
Major

Chord Spelling
1st (G), 3rd (B), 5th (D)

1
2
3
4
5
6
7
8
9
10

I V vi IV in C: Piano

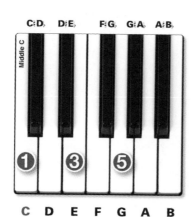

I

C
Major

Chord Spelling
1st (C), 3rd (E), 5th (G)

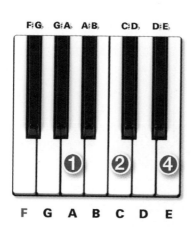

vi

Am
Minor

Chord Spelling
1st (A), ♭3rd (C), 5th (E)

I V vi IV in C: Piano

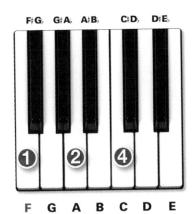

IV

F
Major

Chord Spelling
1st (F), 3rd (A), 5th (C)

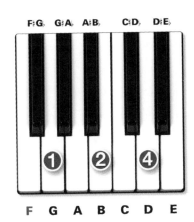

V

G
Major

Chord Spelling
1st (G), 3rd (B), 5th (D)

Examples:
I vi IV V in C

The following pages demonstrate the I vi IV V progression in action in the key of C.

The first example offers a standard use of I vi IV V in C. It begins each bar with a strong full chord, with the notes of the chord echoed in the patterning of melody that follows in the rest of the bar. Apart from the tied notes that create tension, most of the notes in the bar are part of its chord so the results are very tuneful.

The second example on page 270 uses arpeggios (see page 360), or broken chords, even more obviously. The rhythm is consistent again, with each measure running up the notes that make up the chord's basic triad, and then coming back down again. It neatly connects each bar to the next in this way.

Audio example available here:
flametreemusic.com/examples

♩=120

let ring throughout

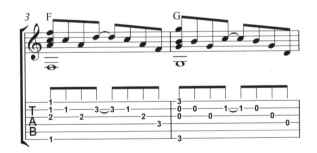

Audio example available here:
flametreemusic.com/examples

♩=120

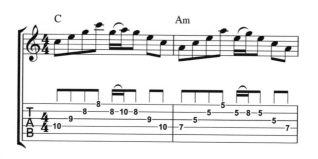

I vi IV V in D
with Example

As shown with previous progressions, the Roman numerals can be transposed to other keys.

To find the progression's chords in D major, we would look at the notes of the D major scale:

D	E	F#	G	A	B	C#
I	ii	iii	IV	V	vi	vii°

So the chords for this progression in D major are:

D	Bm	G	A
I	vi	IV	V
D major	B minor	G major	A major

Chord diagrams for these follow on pages 274–277, and opposite this progression is shown in D.

Audio example available here: flametreemusic.com/examples

♩=170

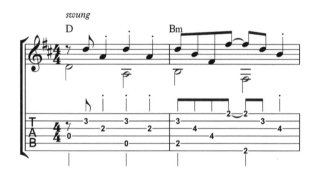

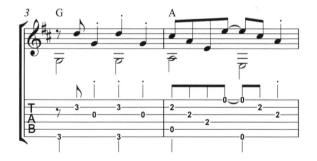

I vi IV V in D: Guitar

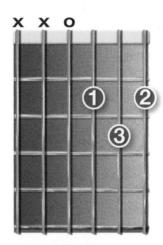

I

D
Major

Chord Spelling
1st (D), 3rd (F♯), 5th (A)

vi

Bm
Minor

Chord Spelling
1st (B), ♭3rd (D), 5th (F♯)

I vi IV V in D: Guitar

IV

G
Major

Chord Spelling
1st (G), 3rd (B), 5th (D)

V

A
Major

Chord Spelling
1st (A), 3rd (C♯), 5th (E)

I vi IV V in D: Piano

I

D
Major

Chord Spelling
1st (D), 3rd (F♯), 5th (A)

vi

Bm
Minor

Chord Spelling
1st (B), ♭3rd (D), 5th (F♯)

I vi IV V in D: Piano

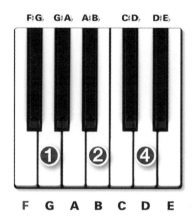

IV

G
Major

Chord Spelling
1st (G), 3rd (B), 5th (D)

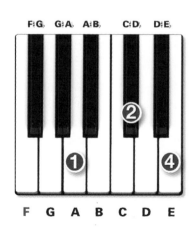

V

A
Major

Chord Spelling
1st (A), 3rd (C♯), 5th (E)

I vi IV V in E
with Example

In E major, the chords needed for the I vi IV V
progression are formed using the notes of the
E major scale:

E	F♯	G♯	A	B	C♯	D♯
I	ii	iii	IV	V	vi	vii°

So the chords for this progression in E major are:

E	C♯m	A	B
I	vi	IV	V
E major	C♯ minor	A major	B major

Chord diagrams for these follow on pages 280–283,
but first you will see opposite this progression
shown in practice in the key of E. On the guitar,
notes shown by the 'x' symbol are to be muted.

Audio example available here:
flametreemusic.com/examples

♩=200-220

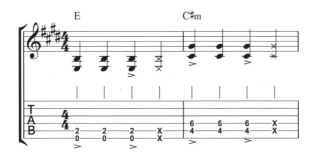

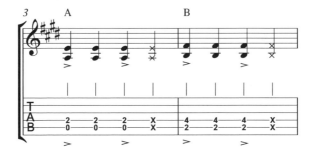

I vi IV V in E: Guitar

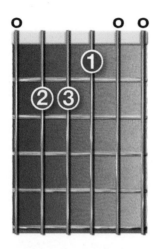

I

E
Major

Chord Spelling
1st (E), 3rd (G♯), 5th (B)

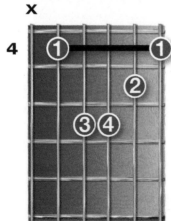

vi

C♯m
Minor

Chord Spelling
1st (C♯), ♭3rd (E), 5th (G♯)

I vi IV V in E: Guitar

IV

A
Major

Chord Spelling
1st (A), 3rd (C♯), 5th (E)

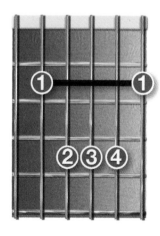

V

B
Major

Chord Spelling
1st (B), 3rd (D♯), 5th (F♯)

I vi IV V in E: Piano

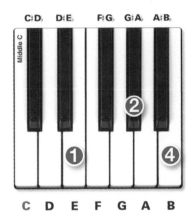

I

E
Major

Chord Spelling
1st (E), 3rd (G♯), 5th (B)

vi

C♯m
Minor

Chord Spelling
1st (C♯), ♭3rd (E), 5th (G♯)

I vi IV V in E: Piano

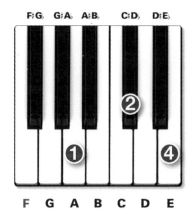

IV

A
Major

Chord Spelling
1st (A), 3rd (C♯), 5th (E)

V

B
Major

Chord Spelling
1st (B), 3rd (D♯), 5th (F♯)

I vi IV V in G
with Example

In G major, the chords needed for the I vi IV V
progression are formed using the notes of the
G major scale:

G	A	B	C	D	E	F$\sharp$
I	ii	iii	IV	V	vi	vii°

So the chords for this progression in G major are:

G	Em	C	D
I	vi	IV	V
G major	E minor	C major	D major

Chord diagrams for these on guitar and piano follow
on pages 286–289, but first you will see opposite a
simple version of this progression shown in practice
in the key of G.

Audio example available here:
flametreemusic.com/examples

♩=120

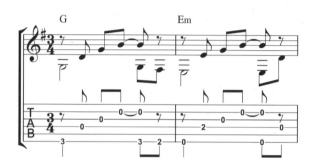

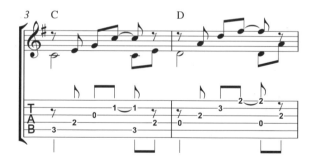

I vi IV V in G: Guitar

I

G
Major

Chord Spelling
1st (G), 3rd (B), 5th (D)

vi

Em
Minor

Chord Spelling
1st (E), ♭3rd (G), 5th (B)

I vi IV V in G: Guitar

IV

C
Major

Chord Spelling
1st (C), 3rd (E), 5th (G)

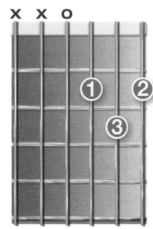

V

D
Major

Chord Spelling
1st (D), 3rd (F♯), 5th (A)

7

I vi IV V in G: Piano

I

G
Major

Chord Spelling
1st (G), 3rd (B), 5th (D)

vi

Em
Minor

Chord Spelling
1st (E), ♭3rd (G), 5th (B)

I vi IV V in G: Piano

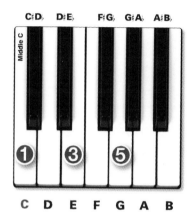

IV

C
Major

Chord Spelling
1st (C), 3rd (E), 5th (G)

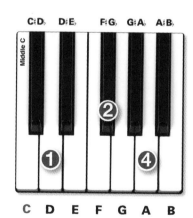

V

D
Major

Chord Spelling
1st (D), 3rd (F♯), 5th (A)

I vi IV V in A
with Example

In A major, the chords needed for the I vi IV V
progression are formed using the notes of the
A major scale:

A	B	C#	D	E	F#	G#
I	ii	iii	IV	V	vi	vii°

So the chords for this progression in A major are:

A	F#m	D	E
I	vi	IV	V
A major	F# minor	D major	E major

Chord diagrams for these on guitar and piano follow
on pages 292–295, but first you will see opposite a
simple version of this progression shown in practice
in the key of A.

Audio example available here:
flametreemusic.com/examples

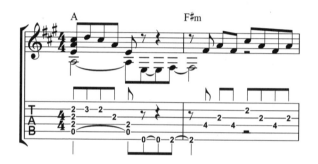

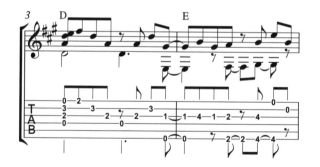

I vi IV V in A: Guitar

I

A
Major

Chord Spelling
1st (A), 3rd (C♯), 5th (E)

vi

F♯m
Minor

Chord Spelling
1st (F♯), ♭3rd (A), 5th (C♯)

I vi IV V in A: Guitar
V

IV

D
Major

Chord Spelling
1st (D), 3rd (F♯), 5th (A)

V

E
Major

Chord Spelling
1st (E), 3rd (G♯), 5th (B)

I vi IV V in A: Piano

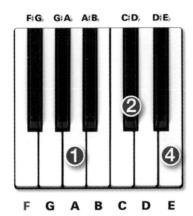

I

A
Major

Chord Spelling
1st (A), 3rd (C♯), 5th (E)

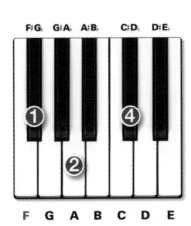

vi

F♯m
Minor

Chord Spelling
1st (F♯), ♭3rd (A), 5th (C♯)

I vi IV V in A: Piano

IV

D
Major

Chord Spelling
1st (D), 3rd (F♯), 5th (A)

V

E
Major

Chord Spelling
1st (E), 3rd (G♯), 5th (B)

Variations

Common types of variations of the I vi IV V
progression include incorporations of 7th chords or
substitutions of one of the chords in the progression
with another. Playing around with the rhythmic
structure, and extending the progression to include
more chords, are also ways to give it a fresh sound.

On the right is an example of the I vi IV V
progression in G, adding 7ths to the first two
chords in the sequence.

On page 298 is another possible variation of the
I vi IV V in C. It introduces passing chords (see page
352) between each of the main chords so that there
are 2 chords per bar. These added chords, and the
use of inversions, allow the bass line to first descend
in steps, and then ascend. For more on moving bass
lines, see pages 346–347.

Audio example available here:
flametreemusic.com/examples

♩=85-95

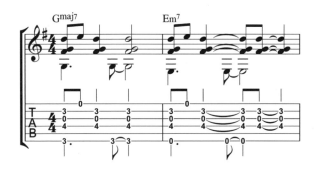

Audio example available here:
flametreemusic.com/examples

♩.= 40

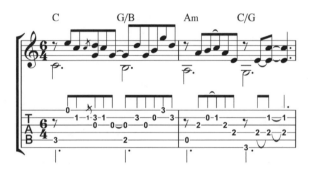

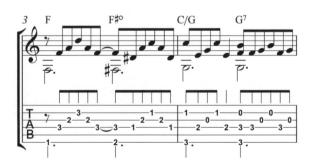

Variation: Adding V7

The most popular form of the I vi IV V progression uses a V7 chord. This is a simple but effective variation of the basic progression.

To recap, the V7 refers to a dominant 7th chord: the initial V triad is major, and the 7th is minor.

In C major, the chord V is G. To find the relevant 7th note to add to that V chord, we take it from the G major scale, where we find the 7th of G is F♯. The V7 chord requires major 3rd and minor 7th intervals, so the B (3rd of G) remains the same but the F♯ is lowered to an F, giving a complete chord of: G, B, D and F.

V7 chords are extremely popular as all the notes are part of the tonic key: all the notes of G7 are in the key of C major. So in the example opposite, all the notes played fall within C major.

Audio example available here:
flametreemusic.com/examples

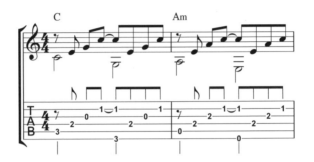

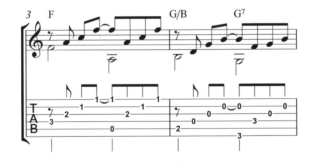

C
Major
Chord Spelling
1st (C), 3rd (E), 5th (G)

Am
Minor
Chord Spelling
1st (A), ♭3rd (C), 5th (E)

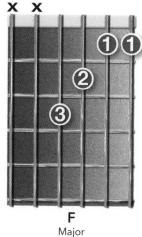

F
Major
Chord Spelling
1st (F), 3rd (A), 5th (C)

G7
Dominant 7th
Chord Spelling
1st (G), 3rd (B), 5th (D), ♭7th (F)

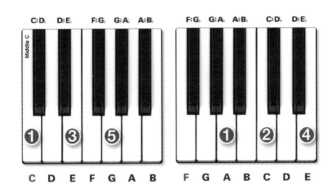

C
Major
Chord Spelling
1st (C), 3rd (E), 5th (G)

Am
Minor
Chord Spelling
1st (A), ♭3rd (C), 5th (E)

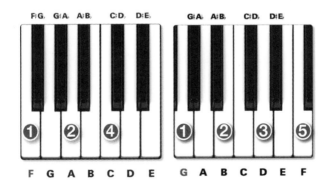

F
Major
Chord Spelling
1st (F), 3rd (A), 5th (C)

G7
Dominant 7th
Chord Spelling
1st (G), 3rd (B), 5th (D), ♭7th (F)

Variation: Chord Substitution with ii

Another common variation of the I vi IV V progression is to substitute the IV chord with ii.

As with the other progressions in this book, the chords needed for the I vi ii V progression can be formed using the major scale.

The example opposite uses G major:

G	A	B	C	D	E	F♯
I	ii	iii	IV	V	vi	vii°

So the chords for this progression in G major are:

G	Em	Am	D
I	vi	ii	V
G major	E minor	A minor	D major

Audio example available here:
flametreemusic.com/examples

♩=90

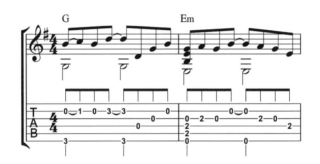

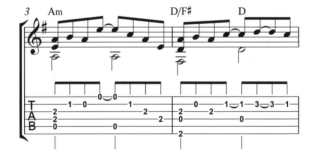

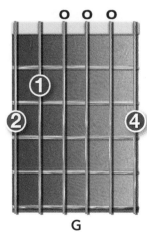

G
Major
Chord Spelling
1st (G), 3rd (B), 5th (D)

Em
Minor
Chord Spelling
1st (E), ♭3rd (G), 5th (B)

Am
Minor
Chord Spelling
1st (A), ♭3rd (C), 5th (E)

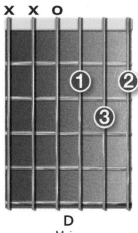

D
Major
Chord Spelling
1st (D), 3rd (F♯), 5th (A)

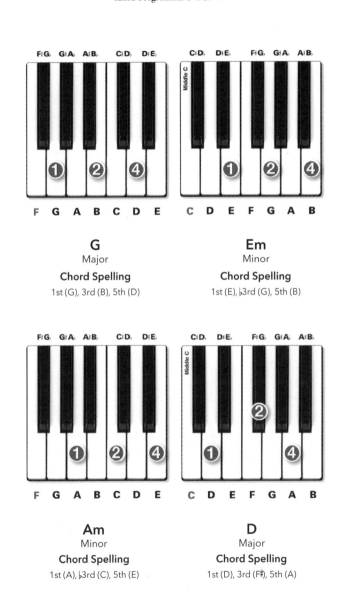

G
Major
Chord Spelling
1st (G), 3rd (B), 5th (D)

Em
Minor
Chord Spelling
1st (E), ♭3rd (G), 5th (B)

Am
Minor
Chord Spelling
1st (A), ♭3rd (C), 5th (E)

D
Major
Chord Spelling
1st (D), 3rd (F♯), 5th (A)

Quick Reference

The I vi IV I progression in the most common keys:

C Major

C	Am	F	G
I	vi	IV	V
1st	6th minor	4th	5th

D Major

D	Bm	G	A
I	vi	IV	V
1st	6th minor	4th	5th

E Major

E	C#m	A	B
I	vi	IV	V
1st	6th minor	4th	5th

G Major

G	Em	C	D
I	vi	IV	V
1st	6th minor	4th	5th

A Major

A	F#m	D	E
I	vi	IV	V
1st	6th minor	4th	5th

8

Going Further

All other chords can be understood as variations or extensions of basic major and minor chords. You can also make your own interpretations of chords by using chord inversions, embellishments and substitutions instead of the original chords. This chapter introduces the many different ways to alter or decorate a chord progression, with examples to show them in practice.

Chord Embellishments

To convert the basic triads into other chords, all
that's normally required is to add a note from
the scale. Sometimes this involves substitution of
another note, as with sus chords, removal of a note,
as with power chords, or simple addition of notes,
as in extended chords: these use notes 'beyond' the
7th note in the scale, such as 9ths, 11ths and 13ths.

Altered chords are another sort of embellishment,
often where one or more of the basic components of
a chord is changed to a note outside the scale, e.g.
sharpening (raising) or flattening (lowering) the 5th.

This section looks at these more advanced chords,
with examples of them in the context of chord
progressions. Chord diagrams for guitar and
piano are given for reference where possible, but
a fuller range for all keys can be found online at
flametreemusic.com.

8

Other Extended Chords: 9ths, 11ths, 13ths

Using extended chords, containing five or six notes, helps to create a rich sound and to extend your chordal vocabulary.

Just as 7th chords are built by adding an extra note to a basic triad, extended chords are built by adding one or more extra notes to a 7th chord.

For example, extensions of major triads use notes from the major scale. We already know Cmaj7:

C   E   G   B

If we add the ninth note of the scale (the same as the 2nd, as the order of notes repeats after 7), we get:

C   E   G   B   D

If we add the eleventh note of the scale (the same as the 4th) we get:

C   E   G   B   D   F

Adding the thirteenth note of the scale (the 6th):

C   E   G   B   D   F   A

The most common types of extended chords are 9ths, 11ths and 13ths. Each can be played in either a major, minor or dominant form:

• Major 9ths, major 11ths, major 13ths are all extensions of major seventh chords.

• Dominant 9ths, dominant 11ths, dominant 13ths are all extensions of dominant seventh chords.

• Minor 9ths, minor 11ths, minor 13ths are all extensions of minor seventh chords.

9ths

Diagrams for C Major 9th on the guitar and piano are shown opposite, but here is a reminder of the notes included for the other types of 9th chords:

Major 9th:

C	E	G	B	D

Dominant 9th:

C	E	G	B♭	D

Minor 9th:

C	E♭	G	B♭	D

Cadd9

Another type of chord that uses the ninth note of the scale is Cadd9. This simply adds the ninth note to a basic triad, giving it a certain warmth.

Cmaj9
Major 9th

Chord Spelling
1st (C), 3rd (E), 5th (G), 7th (B), 9th (D)

8

11ths

Diagrams for C Major 11th on the guitar and piano are shown opposite, but here is a reminder of the notes included for the other types of 11th chords:

Major 11th:

C	E	G	B	D	F

Dominant 11th:

C	E	G	B♭	D	F

Minor 11th:

C	E♭	G	B♭	D	F

On the guitar, the ninth note is normally omitted when playing 11th chords.

On the piano, it's possible to spread the notes of the chord between the left and right hands, as shown opposite.

Cmaj11
Major 9th

Chord Spelling
1st (C), 3rd (E), 5th (G), 7th (B), 9th (D), 11th (F)

13ths

Diagrams for C Major 13th on the guitar and piano are shown opposite, but here is a reminder of the notes included for the other types of 13th chords:

Major 13th:

| C | E | G | B | D | F | A |

Dominant 13th:

| C | E | G | B♭ | D | F | A |

Minor 13th:

| C | E♭ | G | B♭ | D | F | A |

Again, in practice it is not possible to play all these notes on a guitar, therefore some notes (normally the 9th, 11th and sometimes the 5th) are omitted.

On the piano, the large amount of notes can be spread between right and left hands.

Cmaj13
Major 13th

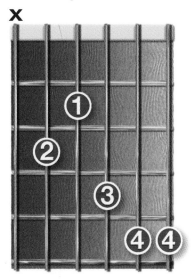

Chord Spelling
1st (C), 3rd (E), 5th (G), 7th (B), 9th (D), 11th (F), 13th (A)

Sus Chords

Some chords are formed by replacing a note rather than adding one. In 'sus' chords, the chord's third is replaced by the fourth note of the major scale in sus4 chords, and by the second note in sus2 chords.

On the guitar, leaving the first string open when playing an open position D major chord shape will give a Dsus2 chord,

D
Major
Chord Spelling
1st (D), 3rd (F♯), 5th (A)

Dsus2
Suspended 2nd
Chord Spelling
1st (D), 2nd (E), 5th (A)

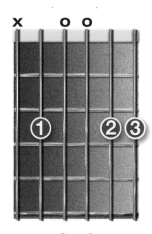

Csus2
Suspended 2nd

Chord Spelling
1st (C), 2nd (D), 5th (G)

Csus4
Suspended 4nd

Chord Spelling
1st (C), 4th (F), 5th (G)

Csus2
Suspended 2nd

Chord Spelling
1st (C), 2nd (D), 5th (G)

Csus4
Suspended 4nd

Chord Spelling
1st (C), 4th (F), 5th (G)

Audio example available here:
flametreemusic.com/examples

♩=100

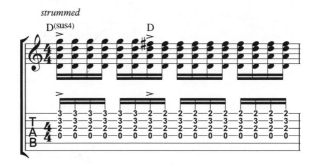

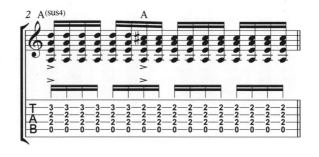

The opposite progression uses sus4 chords. At the start of both bars the sus4 chords resolve to major triads by a half step (4th to 3rd of the chord).

Adding 7ths

It's also possible to play sus chords using 7ths. Below are the diagrams for C7sus4 for both guitar and piano:

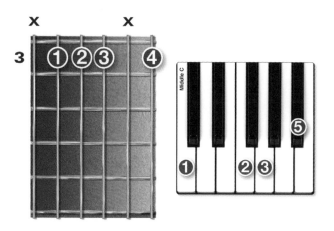

C7sus4
Dominant 7th Suspended 4nd

Chord Spelling
1st (C), 4th (F), 5th (G), ♭7th (B♭)

Power Chords

Power chords unusually do not include a major or minor third; they consist only of the root note and the fifth. They are more common on the guitar, but can be useful on the piano too – for example, when you want to reinforce notes in a chord without committing to a major or minor sound.

They are common in rock music, where the root note and the fifth above it are played on the sixth and fifth, or fifth and fourth strings on the guitar. With the right combination of electric guitar, amp and effects, this powerful sound characterizes hard rock and heavy metal. Often the root note will be duplicated at the octave to create a fuller sound.

Opposite are the chord diagrams for the C5 power chord on the guitar and piano. To hear how these should sound, and for the full range of power chord diagrams, visit flametreemusic.com.

C5
5th (Power Chord)

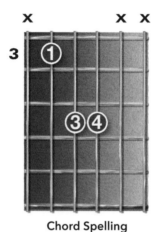

Chord Spelling
1st (C), 5th (G)

6th Chords

6th chords involve the sixth note of the major scale.
For example, in C major, a C6 chord (C major 6th)
would consist of the regular C major triad notes:
C, E, G, plus the sixth note of the major scale: A.

Minor 6th chords are formed in the same way,
with the sixth note of the major scale added to the
minor triad. So Cm6 would be: C, E♭, G, A.

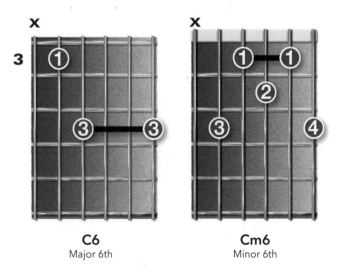

C6
Major 6th

Cm6
Minor 6th

C6
Major 6th

Chord Spelling
1st (C), 3rd (E), 5th (G), 6th (A)

Cm6
Minor 6th

Chord Spelling
1st (C), ♭3rd (E♭), 5th (G), 6th (A)

The below shows a move from Gm to Gm6 chords:

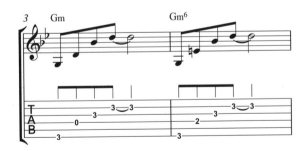

The only difference between these chords is the movement from the 5th (D) to the 6th (E).

Altered Chords

Altered chords provide an ideal method of creating a sense of tension and adding harmonic dissonance to a chord progression.

Raising or lowering the fifth and ninth intervals in chords can also create more colour within a piece. Jazz tunes in particular are based around extended chords (7ths, 9ths, 11ths and 13ths) and their alterations, so it helps to familiarize yourself with these in their various positions.

Here is a reminder of the relevant symbols for some commonly used altered chords:

Diminished triad:	°	(minor thirds stacked on top of each other)
Diminished 7th:	°7	(diminished triad with 7th)
Augmented triad:	+	(5th is raised a semitone, or half step)
Dominant 7th♭5:	7♭5	(5th is flattened/lowered by a semitone)
Dominant 7th♭9:	7♭9	(9th is flattened/lowered by a semitone)
Dominant 7th♯9:	7♯9	(9th is sharpened/raised by a semitone)

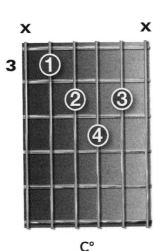

C°
Diminished Triad

Chord Spelling
1st (C), ♭3rd (E♭), ♭5th (G♭)

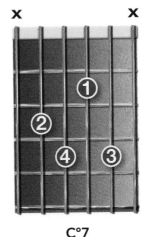

C°7
Diminished 7th

Chord Spelling
1st (C), ♭3rd (E♭), ♭5th (G♭), ♭♭7th (B♭♭)

C°
Diminished Triad

Chord Spelling
1st (C), ♭3rd (E♭), ♭5th (G♭)

C°7
Diminished 7th

Chord Spelling
1st (C), ♭3rd (E♭), ♭5th (G♭), ♭♭7th (B♭♭)

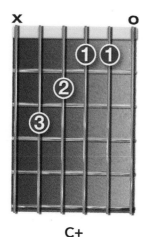

C+
Augmented Triad

Chord Spelling
1st (C), 3rd (E), ♯5th (G♯)

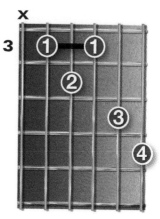

C7-5
Dominant 7th Flattened 5th

Chord Spelling
1st (C), 3rd (E), ♭5th (G♭), ♭7th (B♭)

C+
Augmented Triad

Chord Spelling
1st (C), 3rd (E), ♯5th (G♯)

C7-5
Dominant 7th Flattened 5th

Chord Spelling
1st (C), 3rd (E), ♭5th (G♭), ♭7th (B♭)

C7-9
Dominant 7th Flattened 9th

Chord Spelling
1st (C), 3rd (E), 5th (G), ♭7th (B♭), ♭9th (D♭)

C7+9
Dominant 7th Augmented 9th

Chord Spelling
1st (C), 3rd (E), 5th (G), ♭7th (B♭), ♯9th (D♯)

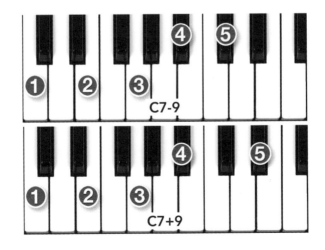

Chord Embellishments in Practice

To consolidate the information given so far, here are a few examples of extended and altered chords in the context of chord progressions.

In the opposite example diminished chords are used in passing, while all other chords are 'diatonic' to C major: they only use notes that fall in the key of C.

On page 336, the example uses 11ths and 7sus4 chords as a way of embellishing a ii V I sequence Page 337 offers an A minor ii V i. Both of the examples on pages 338 and 339 also demonstrate the minor ii V i using altered chords: we see some altered 5ths, a 6th chord with added 9th, and other extensions. Finally, the examples on page 340 and 341 show more altered and extended chords in practice, in different musical styles.

♩=various tempos

Swing

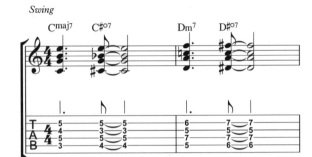

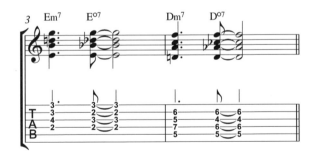

Audio example available here:
flametreemusic.com/examples

♩=100

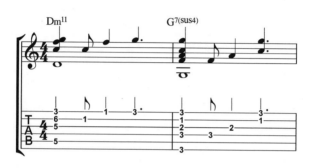

Audio example available here:
flametreemusic.com/examples

♩=90

let ring throughout

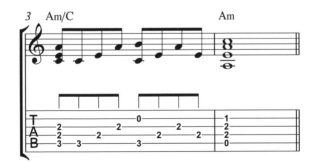

Audio example available here:
flametreemusic.com/examples

♩=100

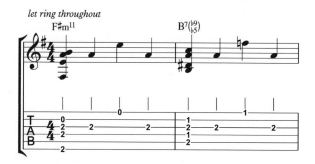

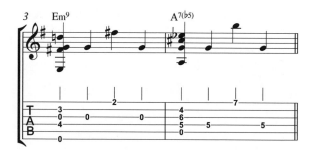

Audio example available here:
flametreemusic.com/examples

♩=100

bossa nova

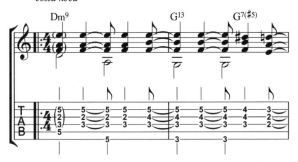

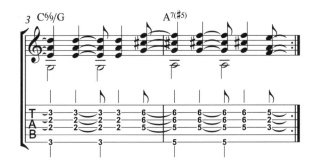

Audio example available here:
flametreemusic.com/examples

♩=100

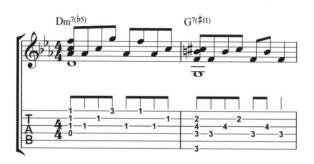

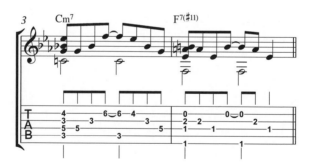

Audio example available here:
flametreemusic.com/examples

♩=115

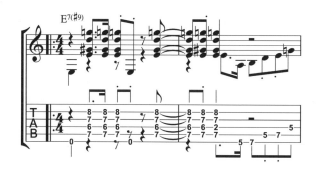

Chord Substitutions and Inversions

As well as switching round chords within a progression, an interesting effect can also be achieved by substituting one chord for another. For example, a major chord might be replaced by its relative minor or a minor chord could be replaced by its relative major.

Chord substitution is particularly common in jazz. It's often done by taking a chord with a dominant seventh note, and replacing it with another chord with a root note a flattened fifth higher – for example, substituting a D♭7 chord for a G minor chord.

For example, with chord substitution, a basic sequence of C-Am-Dm-G could become any of these:

‖ Cmaj9 | Am11 | Dm9 | G13 ‖
‖ Cmaj9 | Am7♯5 | Dm7♭5 | G7♯5♯9 ‖
‖ Cmaj9 | E♭7 | A♭9 | D♭13 ‖

Chord inversions are a versatile way to add variety to an ordinary chord progression. As with the piano diagrams on pages 58–59, the chord diagrams here show the first, second and third inversions for a C chord.

C/E
C Major First Inversion
Chord Spelling
3rd (E), 5th (G), 1st (C)

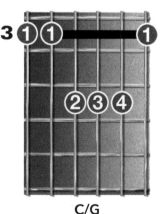

C/G
C Major Second Inversion
Chord Spelling
5th (G), 1st (C), 3rd (E)

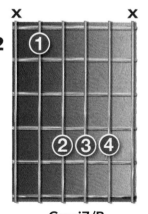

Cmaj7/B
C Major Third Inversion
Chord Spelling
7th (B), 1st (C), 3rd (E), 5th (G)

Relative Minors
and Majors

Relative keys share exactly the same notes but have
a different tonal centre. This can be handy when
moving between chords, or shifting into another key.

C major and A minor, both containing no sharps
or flats, are relative keys. The I, V and IV notes
that would be used frequently in A minor give it a
different sound to the equivalent notes in C major.

A relative minor key's note is always three semitones
below its relative major. Or, put another way,
relative minors are the sixth degree of the major
scale (A is the sixth note of the C major scale).

Opposite is an example of chord substitution using a
relative minor, in this case ending what seems to be
a ii V I progression with A minor instead of C major.

Audio example available here:
flametreemusic.com/examples

♩=150-170

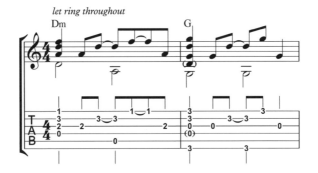

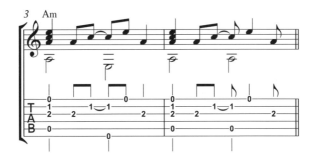

Adding Structure: Moving Bass Lines

A way to add more structure to a progression is to add a moving bass line. To move neatly in small steps usually involves inverted (or slash) chords. There are three main types of moving bassline:

Descending Bassline

Also known as a 'walking bass', a descending bassline moves down in steps. A simple example is shown on page 348, where the inverted G/B chord gives a B in the bass to step between the C and A of adjacent bars. On page 349, you will find another descending bassline using diminished chords.

Ascending Bassline

These go in the opposite direction, stepping up instead of down. A simple example can be found on page 350.

Alternating Bassline

An alternating bass involves a return to the same bass note, usually every other chord, to deliver a strong sense of rhythm. An example can be found on page 351, where the bass moves back and forth between D and A, then B and F♯.

Audio example available here:
flametreemusic.com/examples

♩=175

Audio example available here:
flametreemusic.com/examples

♩=85

let ring throughout

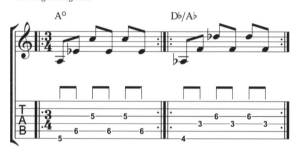

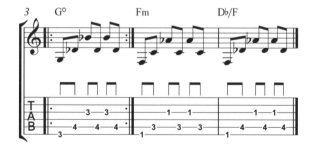

Audio example available here:
flametreemusic.com/examples

♩=175

let ring throughout

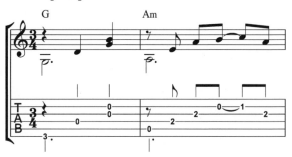

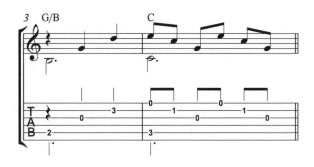

Audio example available here:
flametreemusic.com/examples

♩=140

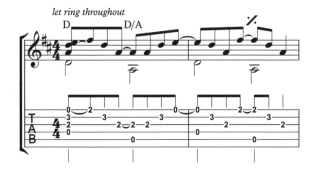

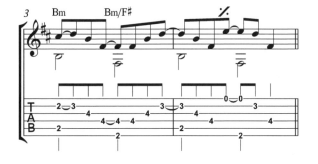

Passing Chords

It's also possible to use chords not technically part of the progression in order to get from one chord to another, or to break up the pattern slightly.

For example, sometimes chord changes are linked by chords a semitone higher or lower (referred to as 'approach chords').

Similarly, as well as the alternating bassline technique described on page 346, it's possible also to alternate the full chords themselves.

Some progressions move forward by returning to the same chord every other chord, which can strengthen a passage and flesh out a basic progression.

A simple example is shown opposite, with a return to the C chord between the F and G chords.

♩=180

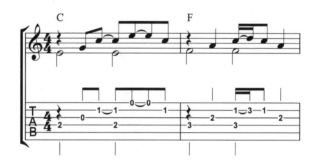

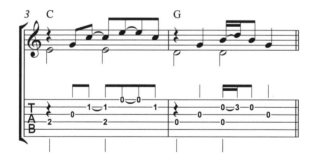

Other Progressions:
The Andalusian Cadence

There are a number of other chord progressions you can use, but we'll look at one more common one: the Andalusian Cadence. This uses vi V IV III chords and is associated with a flamenco style.

The chords for this progression in C major are:

Am	G	F	E
vi	V	IV	III
A minor	G major	F major	E major

In this sequence, to produce the III chord, which in C major is normally minor, the G is sharpened.

An example of it in practice is shown opposite. As can be seen, this progression descends in steps: the chord root notes go from A, to G, to F, to E.

Audio example available here:
flametreemusic.com/examples

♩=100

swing

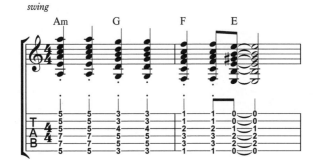

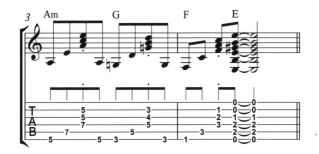

9

Making Music

It's one thing to be able to play through a given chord progression, but creating your own can be a different story. This chapter focuses on the songwriting aspect of playing chord progressions. It will show you how to make existing chord combinations more elaborate, as well as give tips on how to complement progressions with solo-playing.

9

Adding Variety

There are many different ways of playing the same chord, so making a progression sound good is often a case of choosing the combinations and chord formats that best suit your needs at the time. You might want to embellish an existing chord, or add in another chord or different notes here and there.

Developing Riffs

A riff is a short musical phrase that is repeated throughout a song, and is often what hooks a listener in. This is likely to include a chord progression movement of some kind, even if all the chord notes aren't played.

Extended/Altered Chords

Using extended or altered chords is a sure way to add variety to an otherwise basic chord sequence.

Passing Notes

You may want to use the scale you're in to include a few notes between chords. The chromatic scale (see page 376) is a useful scale to know if you'd like to include notes that aren't in the scale too.

Timing and Rhythm

Using chords of different lengths is one way to play with the timing of your progression. A combination of short and long notes, while still keeping a regular rhythm, helps create a distinctive stylistic rhythm.

Syncopation, which shifts the emphasis of beats in a measure away from the obvious timing, is another useful technique to try out.

Rests between chords help add a well-defined rhythm to your progression, giving it musical shape and character.

Arpeggios

An arpeggio is a broken chord in which the notes
of the chord are played individually (rather than
together). As the notes of each arpeggio are taken
from a chord, even in solos they can sound very
tuneful and add colour to a chordal accompaniment.

C major arpeggio

C major chord   C major arpeggio

The opposite example uses arpeggios at the start
of bars 1 and 3 and follows them with alternating
note patterns of broken chords that involve regular
returns to the bass notes.

Audio example available here:
flametreemusic.com/examples

♩=130

let ring throughout

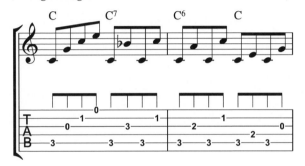

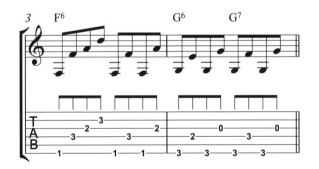

Modulation

Movement to different keys can sometimes be heard, especially in Jazz music. The difference in key is marked by a distinct change in tonality, with confirmation of the new key often reinforced using its primary chords in strong cadences.

If looking out for modulation in a piece of music, watch out for the type and frequency of accidentals. If the same accidentals recur it can suggest movement to a new key, for example to the dominant key or relative minor.

It's common to use chords that are shared by both keys in order to make the transition smoothly. In the opposite example the modulation from C major to G major (movement to the dominant key) is prepared by transitioning from the ii chord of C major (D minor) to the V chord of G major (D major).

$\quad$ =130

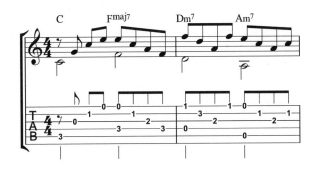

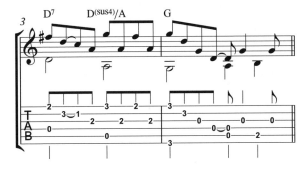

Combining Progressions

While it's important to retain the distinctive feel of a song, that is not to say that progressions cannot be combined. You may find that a repetitive progression throughout a song section can be broken up with a different progression to surprise the listener. It's always worth playing around with different combinations to see what works.

As well as substituting different chords into a progression, substituting whole progressions into a lengthier structure can have a similar effect.

For example, you may want to try substituting a ii V I progression into a twelve-bar blues section, to introduce the added element of the ii chord.

The example in G major opposite combines the first two progressions introduced in this book: first the I V vi IV and then ii V I, ending on a V chord.

Audio example available here:
flametreemusic.com/examples

♩=85

light swing

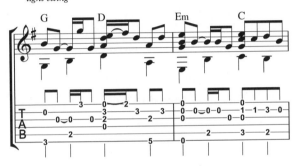

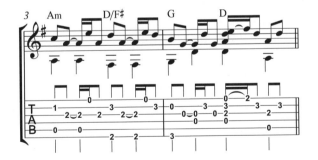

Song Structure

There are no hard and fast rules when it comes to putting a song together, but having a clear basic structure organizes the song and gives obvious markers for where the song is going, which is useful for a listener too. A typical format could be:

Introduction
Verse
Chorus
Verse
Chorus
Middle Eight/Instrumental Break
Verse
Chorus
Chorus
End

The next example demonstrates another typical song structure, using a range of chords and techniques.

Audio example available here:
flametreemusic.com/examples

♩=140

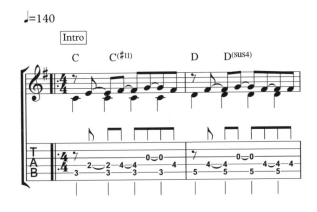

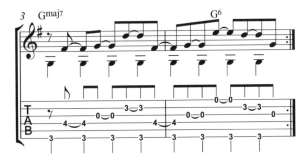

4   Am(add9)

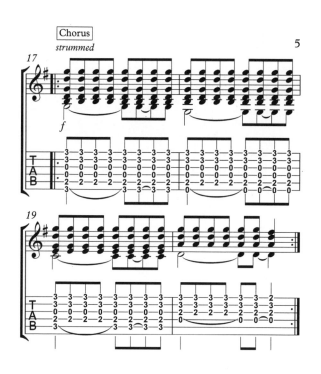

Soloing over Chords

There are many different approaches to soloing over a progression, but the simplest way to learn is to target the root notes of each chord in the progression. Some notes feel 'right' and some don't, often because of their harmonic ties with the chords.

Tips for Soloing

Using Scales

Scales are really suitable for soloing: a lot of typical solos progress up or down a scale, in various forms. Once you've selected a scale to use, this will set the range of notes that will fit with the backing chords. You don't need to play all the notes of the scale, or play them in any set order.

Phrasing

You should always aim to make your solo sound fresh and inventive, rather than scale-like. Some ways to break the patterns are to leave spaces between notes to create short phrases, to use notes of different lengths, and to vary the direction in which you play parts of a scale.

Using Intervals

One thing that always makes a solo sound too scale-like is using notes that are adjacent to each other in a scale. Using interval gaps when playing a scale is a perfect way to break away from this.

Repetition

Repeating short series of notes will help establish phrases that give your solo a sense of structure.

Extra Techniques

On the guitar, string bends, vibrato, slides or slurs will all help give your solo an individual character and will turn it from a melody into a true guitar solo. On the piano, using dynamics and other expressional techniques can be very effective.

Useful Scales

The next pages look at a few common scale types.

The Chromatic Scale

This scale does not relate to a particular key, as it contains every semitone (or half-step) between the starting note and its octave.

Notes from the chromatic scale can be added to introduce notes that are not in the key of the chordal accompaniment. These 'outside' notes are known as 'chromatic' or 'passing' notes, and help provide moments of harmonic tension.

Pentatonic Scales

We've already covered major and minor scales in this book, but there are shorter versions of these that are especially useful for soloing. Pentatonic scales are popular, as they contain fewer notes than the standard seven-note scales so there is less chance of any of the notes clashing with accompanying chords.

Here are the major and minor pentatonic scales in C, though as we have seen with other scales, the basic structures can be applied to all keys.

C Major Pentatonic • Notes: C, D, E, G, A, C

C Minor Pentatonic • Notes: C, E♭, F, G, B♭, C

Other Scale Types: The Blues Scale

Another popular scale is the Blues scale, shown below. This is well suited to dominant seventh chords, especially the I7, IV7 and V7 of the key.

Modes: The Mixolydian Mode

When a major scale begins on a different note, it produces a set of 'modes'. For example, a major scale can be played on its second, or third, or any other of its degrees, in order to produce a different set of interval structures.

When played on its fifth degree, it gives a Mixolydian modal scale. So if C major is played using G as its key note, this is the G Mixolydian scale:

Used in blues, rock, jazz and folk music, this mode can also be thought of as a major scale with a flattened 7th (the F natural in this instance).

10

Resources

Our website flametreemusic.com contains diagrams and audio links for guitar and piano chords and scales, as well as audio for the examples shown in this book. We also have a collection of other music guides that could come in useful if you intend to develop your skills playing and songwriting for the guitar or piano.

10

Other Guides

Here are a few companion titles that could come in useful if you intend to develop your skills playing and songwriting for the guitar or piano.

Guitar Chords

Our bestselling chord book is a comprehensive reference tool for guitarists of any ability. Contains 360 chords, one chord per page, divided by key.

Piano and Keyboard Chords

The equivalent piano chord book includes all the essential piano chords, with a clear diagram and chord spelling for each chord.

Scales for Great Solos

A guide to the most
common scales in all keys,
one scale per page and
links to flametreemusic.com
throughout. Includes tips on
soloing and the best scales to
use for different chords and
music styles.

Guitar Chords Card Pack

A pack of cards introducing common
chord structures and encouraging

experimentation
with popular
chords. One
clear guitar
diagram per card and small
instruction booklet included.

FLAME TREE | PUBLISHING
MUSIC PORTAL

Hear Chords and Scales
FLAMETREEMUSIC.COM

Expert Music Information
FLAMETREEPRO.COM

Sheet Music Playlists
FLAMETREEPIANO.COM

The **FLAME TREE MUSIC PORTAL** brings **chords** and **scales** you can see *and* hear, an **Expert Music search engine** on a wide range of genres, styles, artists and instruments, and free access to **playlists** for our sheet music series.

Other FLAME TREE music books include:

The Jazz and Blues Encyclopedia (Editor: Howard Mandel)
Definitive Opera Encyclopedia (Founding Editor: Stanley Sadie)
Advanced Guitar Chords by Jake Jackson
Beginners Guide to Reading Music by Jake Jackson
Sheet Music for Piano: Scott Joplin by Alan Brown

See our full range of books at **flametreepublishing.com**